MW00636010

TABLE OF CONTENTS

LESSON 2: RECOGNIZING OPPORTUNITIES (CONTINUED)

LESSON 3: IDEAS INTO ACTION 69

LESSON 4: PURSUIT OF KNOWLEDGE 89

LESSON 5: CREATING WEALTH 109

LESSON 6: BUILDING YOUR BRAND 127

Welcome to the Ice House Entrepreneurship Program

As the creators of this course, we hope you find this class intellectually challenging, informative, interactive and fun. Most of all, we hope this course will expose you to a new way of thinking; one that will stir your imagination, ignite your ambition and foster the habits that will enable you to succeed, regardless of the path you choose or where you start.

Here's what you can expect:

The Ice House Entrepreneurship Program is designed to immerse students in the fundamental concepts of an entrepreneurial mindset and the unlimited opportunities it can provide.

By completing this course, you should be able to:

- Identify fundamental aspects of entrepreneurial thinking, compare and contrast entrepreneurial thinking vs. conventional ways of thinking and analyze the outcomes of each.

- Demonstrate critical thinking skills that will enable you to identify and evaluate opportunities within your chosen path.

- Gain the knowledge and develop entrepreneurial skills that will enable you to transform an entrepreneurial idea into a sustainable success.

- Identify and evaluate the most common mistakes entrepreneurs make and learn how to avoid them.

- Develop entrepreneurial attitudes, behaviors and skills that can be applied across disciplines and as a means of personal empowerment.

- Establish goals, identify resources and manage risks in real-world, unpredictable circumstances.

- Identify and interact with local entrepreneurs and business owners within your community who can become potential mentors and/or advisors.

Before you get started, there are a few things you should know:

Entrepreneurship development is not a spectator sport. The Ice House Entrepreneurship Program is designed to be interactive and experiential. While traditional classroom learning can play an important role, the core experience should include interaction with real-world entrepreneurs, hands-on experience and exposure to economic risks. We encourage you to share your knowledge and experience with your classmates, interact with local entrepreneurs and apply what you learn in real-world circumstances.

The more you put into the course, the more benefit you are likely to receive.

The Ice House Entrepreneurship Program also includes access to a vibrant online entrepreneurial learning community designed to communicate and interact with your peers as well as your instructor. Students and teachers can share resources, post articles and create discussions in public forums or in private groups.

See your instructor on how to gain access to the online learning community.

Here's how the course works:

The Ice House Entrepreneurship Program is divided into individual lessons. Within each lesson there are five basic elements:

1. **A narrated chalkboard presentation** that combines basic bullet-point text and simple diagrams with video interview segments featuring successful real-world entrepreneurs. Similar to a classroom lecture, the narrated chalkboard presentations range from 40 to 90 minutes in length. The narrated presentations are divided into individual chapters that enable you to pause and discuss as you go.

2. **A true/false lesson review** to help insure knowledge awareness and comprehension.

3. **Chapter-specific discussion topics** designed to foster student-to-student interaction and develop critical thinking skills. Participation is strongly encouraged.

4. A reflection and response assignment designed to encourage you to reflect on what you have learned and how it can be applied to your individual circumstances.

5. Application assignments designed to immerse you in real-world experiences that will encourage you to develop entrepreneurial skills. The application assignments are designed for both individual and small group activities. Students are encouraged to share what they learn with fellow participants, either in class or in the online learning community.

Note: At the end of this course you will be asked to create a personal vision statement designed to help you clarify your priorities and goals. You will also participate in an opportunity discovery process that will enable you to identify and evaluate entrepreneurial opportunities.

To get the most out of this course, we encourage you to:

- **Take notes.** As you view the narrated chalkboards, you are encouraged to take notes in the "Chalkboard Notes" section provided in this workbook.

- **Take your time.** There is a lot of information to absorb. Take time to reflect on what you have learned and how it can be applied to your own life. Your individual reflections will form the basis of your personal vision statement at the end of the course.

- **Complete all of the assignments.** They are designed to foster real-world application of the core content. And, like anything else, the more effort you put in, the more meaningful your experience will be.

- **Share what you have learned with others.** Peer-to-peer learning is a powerful tool. Sharing your knowledge will also help you retain the knowledge you have gained.

- **See your instructor for additional details** regarding project due dates, grading requirements and other course details.

Introduction Lesson

Overview

The introductory lesson offers a brief overview of the eight life lessons and an introduction to several of the Ice House Entrepreneurs. We will also take a look beneath the surface to examine some of the most commonly held myths about what it really takes to succeed as an entrepreneur. Lastly, we will introduce you to some basic concepts that are essential to understand.

1. What you will learn
Chapter one provides a brief description of each of the eight life lessons.

2. Introduction to the Ice House Entrepreneurs
In chapter two, we'll introduce several of the Ice House Entrepreneurs who will describe in their own words the opportunities they found, the challenges they faced and the valuable lessons they learned along the way.

3. Unravelling the mystery
Are entrepreneurs born with a unique ability or is entrepreneurship something that we can learn? In chapter three, we'll examine the myths and explore the reality of what it really takes to become a successful entrepreneur.

4. Mindset defined
What exactly is a mindset? The mindset may be the most important aspect of entrepreneurship, yet it may also be the most often overlooked and widely misunderstood. In chapter four, we'll define the term in a way that is actionable to an aspiring entrepreneur.

Introduction Lesson - Chalkboard Notes

Introduction Lesson - Chalkboard Notes

_____

_____

_____

_____

_____

_____

_____

_____

_____

_____

_____

_____

Introduction Lesson - Chalkboard Notes

_____

_____

_____

_____

_____

_____

_____

_____

_____

_____

_____

_____

Name: _____ Date: _____

Introduction Lesson - Review

This true/false lesson review will help ensure knowledge awareness and comprehension.

True or False - circle one

Chapter 3: Unravelling the mystery

1. Entrepreneurs have become the engines that are now driving our economy, yet their abilities remain shrouded in mystery and our perception of what it actually takes to succeed as an entrepreneur may be inaccurate or out of date. **T or F**

2. Much of what entrepreneurs know, they learned by following a carefully planned step-by-step process. **T or F**

3. Tacit knowledge is gained through a formal learning process and is easy to convey in a textbook. **T or F**

4. Those who possess tacit knowledge are often unaware of the knowledge they possess or how it can be valuable to others. **T or F**

Chapter 4: Mindset defined

5. A mindset is a set of beliefs and assumptions that influence our decisions and our behaviors. **T or F**

6. Our mindset often becomes an established set of beliefs, one that often limits us to familiar ways of thinking and acting. **T or F**

7. A belief is the same as a fact. **T or F**

8. Those with an entrepreneurial mindset tend to approach life as a series of experiments rather than a set of circumstances over which they have no control. **T or F**

Introduction Lesson - Discussions

The discussions are designed to foster peer-to-peer interaction while enabling participants to connect their prior knowledge with the course material.

Chapter 1: What you will learn

1. Why are you taking this course? What do you hope to learn?

   _____

   _____

2. What, if any prior entrepreneurial experience do you have?

   _____

   _____

3. Of the eight lessons, which is the most interesting to you? Why?

   _____

   _____

4. Of the eight lessons, which do you feel you understand the best? Which do you feel you understand the least?

   _____

   _____

5. Do you think entrepreneurship is an innate ability that we are born with or is it learned? Why?

   _____

   _____

6. Do you want to become an entrepreneur? Why? Why not?

   _____

   _____

7. What do you see as the greatest obstacle(s) to becoming an entrepreneur?

_____

_____

Chapter 2: Introduction to Ice House Entrepreneurs

1. Which of the entrepreneurs introduced were the most interesting to you? Why?

    _____

    _____

2. Do you know an entrepreneur personally? If so, can you describe their startup story? What was their idea? How did they get started? Was it something that had never been done before?

    _____

    _____

3. Describe the advantages they had as well as the obstacles they faced. How did they overcome them?

    _____

    _____

Chapter 3: Unravelling the mystery

1. Why were entrepreneurs largely ignored in the past? Why has this changed?

    _____

    _____

2. When you think of an entrepreneur, does a particular individual come to mind?

    _____

    _____

3. What characteristics do they bring to mind? Can those characteristics be learned?

_____

_____

4. What do you think is required to succeed as an entrepreneur? (Brains, luck, money, risk tolerance, patentable idea, etc.)

_____

_____

Chapter 4: Mindset defined

1. What is a mindset? Why is it important to becoming an entrepreneur?

_____

_____

2. What factors influence our mindset?

_____

_____

3. How does our mindset affect the choices we make?

_____

_____

4. How did Rodney Walker's environment shape his mindset? How did his mindset influence his behavior?

_____

_____

5. How do our beliefs and assumptions about the world impact our decisions?

_____

_____

6. How do our beliefs and assumptions about ourselves affect our decisions?

_____

_____

7. How can our beliefs keep us stuck?

_____

_____

8. Describe an example of a person or group of people who cling to their beliefs even when those beliefs may not support their own self-interest.

_____

_____

9. Why would we want to change our mindset?

_____

_____

10. Why is it important to approach life as a series of experiments rather than established facts?

_____

_____

Final Introduction Lesson Discussion
How does this concept answer the guiding questions?

1. How do entrepreneurs with limited resources identify and pursue opportunities?
2. How do those who have nothing, create something?

Introduction Lesson - Discussion Notes

_____

_____

_____

_____

_____

_____

_____

_____

_____

_____

_____

_____

_____

Introduction Lesson - Discussion Notes

_____

_____

_____

_____

_____

_____

_____

_____

_____

_____

_____

_____

Introduction Lesson - Discussion Notes

_____

_____

_____

_____

_____

_____

_____

_____

_____

_____

_____

_____

Reflection and Response Assignments

The reflection and response assignments provide an opportunity to reflect on what you have learned and how you can apply the knowledge in a way that will empower you to accomplish your goals. The focus of peer-to-peer learning should encourage students to share the beliefs and assumptions that either enhanced or inhibited their abilities to achieve their desired results.

As you work through each lesson, you will begin to develop a personal vision statement that will help you clarify your objectives and stay focused on your goals. Your answers should be submitted in the response section provided below. Your answers can be as long or as short as you like. Remember; the more effort you put into the assignments, the more benefit you are likely to receive. You are also encouraged to share your reflections in the online learning community.

Introduction Lesson - Reflection and Response Assignment

How do entrepreneurs with limited resources identify opportunities that the rest of us seem to overlook? What is it that enables them to transform a simple idea into a sustainable success, regardless of where they start? Are they born with a unique ability or is entrepreneurship something we can learn?

Name: _____ **Date:** _____

Why are you taking this course? What do you hope to learn? Which of the featured entrepreneurs was most interesting to you and why? What do you think it takes to become a successful entrepreneur?

_____

_____

_____

_____

_____

_____

_____

_____

_____

_____

_____

_____

Name: _____ **Date:** _____

Response:
What was the most important aspect of this lesson for you? How does your mindset influence your behavior? How will an entrepreneurial mindset enable you to accomplish your goals?

_____

_____

_____

_____

_____

_____

_____

_____

_____

_____

Application Assignments

Application Assignments are designed to enhance participation and engage you in experiential learning exercises that will enable you to apply the core concepts in the real world.

Application Assignments will enable you to identify and evaluate potential opportunities in real-world circumstances. This is also known as the Opportunity Discovery Process. Starting with where you are, what you have and who you know, the Application Assignments are action oriented activities designed to stimulate self-directed learning, critical thinking, collaboration, effective problem solving and other entrepreneurial skills.

You are encouraged to share your interactions and observations through frequent classroom presentations as well as in the online learning community.

Introduction Lesson - Application Assignments

How do entrepreneurs with limited resources identify opportunities that the rest of us seem to overlook? What is it that enables them to transform a simple idea into a sustainable success, regardless of where they start? Are they born with a unique ability or is entrepreneurship something we can learn?

- Log in to online learning community and create your profile. Be sure to add your location on the member map and introduce yourself to the group. (See your instructor for information about how to gain access to the online learning community.)

- Read **Chapter 1: Choice** in *Who Owns the Ice House?*

- **Online Participants Only:** Complete the online student survey.

Lesson 1: The Power to Choose

Uncle Cleve's Message

The ability to choose the way we respond to our circumstances is perhaps the greatest power we have. It is a power that Clifton's uncle, Cleve Mormon, demonstrated throughout his life:

> • *He had not a single advantage to claim over any of the others within his community and most were exposed to the same opportunities, yet many were simply blinded by their beliefs. He had no financial advantage— Uncle Cleve did not come from a wealthy family nor did he have access to venture capital investors or credit from a local bank. At that time, most banks would not even consider lending money to an African American. Uncle Cleve was an ordinary man whose only advantage was his mindset.*

> • *He had no intellectual or academic advantage—Uncle Cleve was a simple man of average intelligence who displayed no particular genius. Although he could read and write and he understood basic math, he had no specialized knowledge, technical training, or other skills to set him apart. His formal education likely did not extend beyond the sixth grade.*

> • *He had no political advantage—Uncle Cleve had no government contracts, inside knowledge, or special connections that enabled him to succeed. Uncle Cleve was an ordinary man whose only advantage was his mindset, a mindset that enabled him to choose a different life that allowed him to triumph over adversity as an entrepreneur. It was his mindset that awakened his curiosity and opened his eyes to the world around him. It was his mindset that enabled him to recognize opportunities that others could not see. It was his mindset that ignited within him a desire and determination that empowered him to triumph over adversity and succeed as an entrepreneur. Ultimately, it was his mindset that set his spirit free.*

Lesson 1: The Power to Choose

Overview

Life is not a lottery. The ability to choose the way we respond to our circumstances is fundamental to an entrepreneurial mindset. Using real-world examples, participants learn to recognize how choices rather than circumstances will ultimately shape our lives.

1. Influence
In chapter one, we'll learn how our environment can influence our mindset and the decisions we make - decisions that may be holding us back.

2. React vs. Respond
Chapter two examines the difference between a reaction and a response. Students learn how entrepreneurs respond to their circumstances rather than react.

3. Locus of Control
Chapter three introduces the concept of an internal vs. an external locus of control. In this chapter, we will examine both perspectives and discuss the outcomes of each.

4. Vision: The Power to Choose
In chapter four, we will learn how entrepreneurs use their imagination and vision to access the greatest power they have - *the power to choose*.

Lesson 1: The Power to Choose - Chalkboard Notes

_____

_____

_____

_____

_____

_____

_____

_____

_____

_____

_____

_____

_____

Lesson 1: The Power to Choose - Chalkboard Notes

_____

_____

_____

_____

_____

_____

_____

_____

_____

_____

_____

_____

Lesson 1: The Power to Choose - Chalkboard Notes

_____

_____

_____

_____

_____

_____

_____

_____

_____

_____

_____

_____

Name: _____ Date: _____

Lesson 1: The Power to Choose - Review

True or False - circle one

Chapter 1: Influence

1. We often make important choices based on limited information, unchallenged assumptions or outdated beliefs. **T or F**

2. Our environment and the collective mindset of others has very little influence over the choices we make. **T or F**

Chapter 2: React vs. Respond

3. A reaction is often experienced as an impulse rather than a conscious choice. **T or F**

4. Reactions are learned patterns of thoughts, feelings and actions that cannot be controlled. **T or F**

5. In the same way that we might react to a specific event such as a rude driver, we can also react to our circumstances in ways that lack conscious choice or deliberate intent. **T or F**

Chapter 3: Locus of Control

6. When we respond, we think about what we want to have happen, we are making a conscious choice. **T or F**

7. Those with an external locus of control believe that luck, fate, circumstances or powerful others will determine the outcome of their lives. **T or F**

8. Those with an internal locus of control tend to see themselves as the source of control. **T or F**

9. Those with an internal locus of control tend to focus their time and energy on things that will improve their lives. **T or F**

Chapter 4: The Power to Choose

10. By creating a vision, we are exercising our power to choose.   T or F

11. A vision can be a distraction - one that often prevents us from dealing with the day-to-day necessities of life.   T or F

Chapter 4: The Power to Choose - Part 2

12. A vision should be defined by the resources that are currently available and include a detailed account of exactly how you intend to accomplish your goals. T or F

Lesson 1: The Power to Choose - Discussions

Chapter 1: Influence

1. How did Rodney Walker describe the collective mindset of his peers? How did that influence his decisions and limit his choices?

    _____

    _____

2. How was Ted Moore influenced by his environment? What assumptions did he make based on his environment?

    _____

    _____

3. What choice did Palwasha Siddiqi make that was different from others within her community? How did she respond to the pressure to give up on her dream of becoming an entrepreneur?

    _____

    _____

Chapter 1: Influence - Part 2

1. Describe an example of social or environmental influence in our culture today.

    _____

    _____

2. How would you interpret the saying "it takes money to make money"?

    _____

    _____

3. Do you see the lack of money as an obstacle? Have you ever rejected an opportunity due to a lack of money?

_____

_____

4. Describe an example of how our beliefs about the world may limit our choices.

_____

_____

5. Are those beliefs facts or are they unchallenged assumptions?

_____

_____

6. How does the belief in our own powerlessness hold us back?

_____

_____

Chapter 2: React vs. Respond

1. What did Dr. Frankl mean by 'space' when he said "Between stimulus and response there is a space. In that space is our power to choose our response. In our response lies our growth and our freedom."

_____

_____

2. Describe the difference between a reaction and a response.

_____

_____

3. Describe an example of someone who is reacting to their circumstances.

_____

_____

4. Describe an example of how you could respond to the same set of circumstances.

_____

_____

5. Describe the underlying beliefs and assumptions that might cause us to react.

_____

_____

6. Describe the underlying beliefs and assumptions that might cause us to respond.

_____

_____

7. How can responding rather than reacting empower you?

_____

_____

8. As Dr. Frankl said, "Our greatest power lies in the awareness of the existence of choices, regardless of the situation or context." Why is this important to an entrepreneurial mindset?

_____

_____

Chapter 3: Locus of Control

1. Describe the difference between a person with an internal and an external locus of control.

_____

_____

2. Describe the underlying beliefs and assumptions of each.

_____

_____

3. How were Rodney Walker, Ted Moore and Palwasha Saddiqi influenced by an external locus of control?

_____

_____

4. What events shifted their perspective to an internal locus of control?

_____

_____

5. How did their shift in perspective influence their behavior?

_____

_____

6. Provide an example of a situation or circumstances that we cannot control.

_____

_____

7. Provide an example of how someone might react to this situation or circumstance.

_____

_____

8. Provide an example of how they might respond.

_____

_____

9. Why is it important to understand the difference?

_____

_____

10. Why is this important to an entrepreneurial mindset?

_____

_____

11. Describe the circumstances or events that influenced David Petite to develop an internal locus of control.

_____

_____

12. Describe a specific belief that demonstrates an internal locus of control.

_____

_____

13. What happens when we focus our time and attention on things we can change rather than things we cannot?

_____

_____

14. How does it influence our decisions?

_____

_____

15. How might this shift in awareness alter the course of our lives?

_____

_____

Chapter 4: Vision - The Power to Choose

1. Why is having a vision important to an entrepreneurial mindset?

_____

_____

39

2. How does having a vision influence our choices?

_____

_____

3. How does a vision influence our behavior?

_____

_____

4. How do you interpret the concept of time as currency?

_____

_____

Chapter 4: Vision - The Power to Choose - Part 2

1. Provide an example of how our beliefs about the world around us may influence our vision or the goals we set for ourselves.

_____

_____

2. Provide an example of how our beliefs about our own abilities may influence our vision or the goals we set for ourselves.

_____

_____

3. Provide an example of spending versus investing our time.

_____

_____

4. How does an entrepreneur's ability to focus their time and attention on their vision separate them from the crowd?

_____

_____

5. What are the underlying beliefs and assumptions that encourage entrepreneurs to focus their time and attention on their goals?

_____

_____

6. What are the underlying beliefs and assumptions that might discourage a person from establishing a vision or a goal?

_____

_____

7. How did Brian Scudamore harness the power of vision?

_____

_____

8. How did his vision progress over time?

_____

_____

9. Describe some of the self-doubts he encountered along the way.

_____

_____

10. Did he limit his vision by the resources and abilities that were currently known?

_____

_____

11. How is creating a vision or a goal exercising our power to choose?

_____

_____

12. How did Uncle Cleve exercise his power to choose?

_____

_____

13. Was he influenced by an internal or an external locus of control?

_____

_____

How does this concept answer the guiding questions?

1. How do entrepreneurs with limited resources identify and pursue opportunities?
2. How do those who have nothing, create something?

Lesson 1: The Power to Choose - Discussion Notes

_____

_____

_____

_____

_____

_____

_____

_____

_____

Lesson 1: The Power to Choose - Discussion Notes

_____

_____

_____

_____

_____

_____

_____

_____

_____

_____

_____

_____

Lesson 1: The Power to Choose - Discussion Notes

_____

_____

_____

_____

_____

_____

_____

_____

_____

_____

_____

_____

_____

Name: _____ Date: _____

Lesson 1: The Power to Choose - Reflection and Response

Life is not a lottery. The ability to choose the way we respond to our circumstances is fundamental to an entrepreneurial mindset.

Reflection:
What does success look like for you? If you could choose the life you want, describe the life you would choose. What are the most important things you want to make happen in your life and your career? What is the single greatest obstacle that is preventing you from accomplishing your goals?

_____

_____

_____

_____

_____

_____

_____

_____

_____

Name: _____ **Date:** _____

What was the most important aspect of this lesson for you? More importantly, how will it change your behavior in a way that will move you closer to your goals?

_____

_____

_____

_____

_____

_____

_____

_____

_____

_____

Lesson 1: The Power to Choose - Application Assignments

Life is not a lottery. The ability to choose the way we respond to our circumstances is fundamental to an entrepreneurial mindset.

Prepare an "Icebreaker" introduction. Your Icebreaker introduction provides an opportunity for a more in-depth introduction. Your Icebreaker can be a scripted or unscripted presentation.

Share some of the highlights from your reflection and response assignment:

■ Why did you choose to take this course and what do you hope to learn?

■ What is the biggest barrier that is preventing you from accomplishing your goals?

■ Which of the featured entrepreneurs was most interesting to you and why?

■ What do you think it takes to become a successful entrepreneur?

Share any prior knowledge or experience you may have as an entrepreneur:

■ Do you personally know any entrepreneurs? If so, provide a brief description.

■ How has that person influenced your thinking?

■ Do you think entrepreneurs are born with a unique ability or is entrepreneurship something we can learn?

■ Do you have an idea for a business? If so, briefly describe your idea.

■ Describe your greatest strength that may help you as an entrepreneur. *For example, you might say that you are persuasive and not afraid to approach people.*

■ Describe your greatest weakness that may hinder you as an entrepreneur. *For example, you might say that you are not a detail oriented person or that you are not good at math.*

■ Do you prefer to work in a group or as part of a team or would you prefer to work alone? Why?

Read **Chapter 2: Opportunity** in *Who Owns the Ice House?*

Lesson 2: Recognizing Opportunities

Uncle Cleve's Message

Uncle Cleve was a problem solver. He understood that problems were opportunities and that if he could identify problems and find solutions for other people, he would prosper as well. He did not set out simply to make money for himself. He paid attention to the world around him, staying attuned to problems and issues that others complained about—especially the issues that he could address or improve. He was curious and his mind was constantly engaged, perpetually searching for solutions to the problems of others within his community. Everyone in Glen Allan needed ice. Uncle Cleve's solutions were not complex; much like delivering coal or wood or fixing cars, these issues did not involve revolutionary new technology or highly specialized knowledge. They did not require large sums of money or access to power and privilege. They were simple solutions to commonplace problems, solutions that were propelled by common sense, solutions rooted in reliability, good service—and a willingness to work long hours and take small risks.

Lesson 2: Recognizing Opportunities

Overview

Problems are often opportunities in disguise. Entrepreneurs are problem solvers and the secret to their success lies in their ability to identify problems and find solutions. In this lesson, we will learn how to identify problems and use knowledge and experience to find solutions.

1. In search of opportunity
In chapter one, we'll examine the importance of balancing the "right" idea with our abilities as an entrepreneur.

2. Problems are opportunities
In chapter two, we'll examine some of the fundamental concepts and the underlying assumptions that enable entrepreneurs to identify opportunities regardless of their circumstances.

3. Simple solutions
In chapter three, we'll see how entrepreneurs with limited resources transform simple solutions into successful, new ventures.

4. Opportunistic adaptation
In chapter four, we'll describe the process of opportunistic adaptation. We'll see how entrepreneurs often uncover unforeseen opportunities through the process of interaction and observation, experimentation and adaptation.

5. Prior work experience
In chapter five, we'll discuss where to look for opportunities. While some set out in search of a big idea, we'll see how entrepreneurs learn to identify opportunities in their own back yard.

6. Enthusiastic and somewhat inexperienced

Contrary to popular belief, we do not need to be an "expert" to become an entrepreneur. In chapter six, we'll see how successful entrepreneurs overcome their lack of experience to succeed.

7. Inventor as entrepreneur

In chapter seven, we'll learn directly from a very successful inventor and entrepreneur who will describe the process of identifying problems and finding solutions.

Lesson 2: Recognizing Opportunities - Chalkboard Notes

_____

_____

_____

_____

_____

_____

_____

_____

_____

Lesson 2: Recognizing Opportunities - Chalkboard Notes

_____

_____

_____

_____

_____

_____

_____

_____

_____

_____

_____

_____

_____

Lesson 2: Recognizing Opportunities - Review

True or False - circle one

Chapter 1: In search of opportunity

1. Coming up with a good idea is more important than your abilities as an entrepreneur.
   T or F

Chapter 2: Problems are opportunities

2. Problem solving is a rare ability that some people have and others do not.
   T or F

3. Becoming an entrepreneur requires a formulaic and structured approach to problem solving. **T or F**

Chapter 3: Simple solutions

4. Brian Scudamore had years of experience in the trash hauling business before starting 1-800 GOT-JUNK. **T or F**

Chapter 4: Opportunistic adaptation

5. Success as an entrepreneur usually requires venture capital and an experienced management team. **T or F**

6. Rather than in-depth planning, entrepreneurs often uncover larger more attractive opportunities once they are in motion. **T or F**

7. The process of opportunistic adaptation can uncover opportunities that would be otherwise difficult to recognize. **T or F**

8. Through careful planning, Lydia Gutierrez and her late husband Richard, identified an opportunity that enabled them to achieve success quickly.
   T or F

Chapter 5: Prior work experience

9. Entrepreneurs often encounter opportunities through a prior work experience.
   T or F

10. Keith Kokal learned to identify opportunities while working at an ordinary job.
    T or F

Chapter 6: Enthusiastic and somewhat inexperienced

11. Successful entrepreneurs should have years of experience in a particular field before deciding to start a business.   **T or F**

12. Inexperience can be an advantage that enables entrepreneurs to identify opportunities that "experts" overlook.   **T or F**

13. Carey Mobius had very little experience when he took over his family's business.
    T or F

Chapter 8: Fatal assumptions

14. Understanding the technical work of a business will prepare you to run a business that does that type of technical work.   **T or F**

15. Entrepreneurs tend to be high stakes gamblers who are willing to bet everything on their ideas.   **T or F**

16. Successful entrepreneurs identify the problem first, then create a solution.
    T or F

17. If your idea is good, success should be fairly easy.   **T or F**

18. Selecting a business that is close to home and does not require new skills is an advisable approach for an inexperienced entrepreneur.   **T or F**

Lesson 2: Recognizing Opportunities - Discussions

Chapter 1: In search of opportunity

1. It's been said that entrepreneurship is 1% inspiration and 99% perspiration. What do you think is more important: the idea or the entrepreneur's ability to execute on their idea? Why?

    _____
    _____

2. Describe an example of a simple idea that was well executed. Describe an example of a good idea that was not well executed.

    _____
    _____

Chapter 2: Problems are opportunities

1. How do entrepreneurs create success by solving problems?

    _____
    _____

2. How does the assumption that problems are potential opportunities empower an entrepreneur?

    _____
    _____

3. Describe the underlying beliefs and assumptions that encourage this belief.

    _____
    _____

4. Describe the underlying beliefs and assumptions that discourage this belief.

    _____
    _____

5. Describe the difference between convergent and divergent thinking. Provide an example of each.

_____

_____

6. Discuss the importance of divergent thinking to an entrepreneurial mindset.

_____

_____

7. What problem was Brian Scudamore solving for his customers? What was the "secret" to his success?

_____

_____

8. Identify a successful business. Explain the problem they are solving for their customers.

_____

_____

Chapter 3: Simple solutions

1. While we so often hear of the high-tech entrepreneurs who invent groundbreaking new technologies that change the world, the vast majority of successful entrepreneurs do not invent breakthrough technologies. Describe an example of a successful business that offers a simple solution to an everyday problem.

_____

_____

_____

1. Rather than searching for big ideas that involve breakthrough technologies, the vast majority of entrepreneurs pursue opportunities that are small and highly uncertain. Even entrepreneurs like Sam Walton and Bill Gates start out initially pursuing small and uncertain opportunities. It is only once they are in motion that they discover a larger opportunity, an opportunity that would otherwise be invisible. Describe the concept of opportunistic adaptation and how it differs from in-depth planning.

    _____

    _____

    _____

2. How did Brian Scudamore identify an unforeseen opportunity through the process of opportunistic adaptation?

    _____

    _____

3. How did Lydia Gutierrez and her husband identify unforeseen opportunities through the process of opportunistic adaptation?

    _____

    _____

4. What skills were required?

    _____

    _____

1. As we know, rather than a random moment of inspiration, successful entrepreneurs like Keith Kokal often pursue small and highly uncertain niche opportunities - *opportunities they encounter while working at a traditional job.* Have you encountered an opportunity while at work that you were able to solve?

    _____

    _____

2. Describe the problem as well as the solution. Were you encouraged to pursue a solution? Did you view the problem as an opportunity? How did Keith Kokal's experience at the auto parts store help him identify other opportunities?

    _____

    _____

3. What were the underlying beliefs and assumptions that influenced his behavior?

    _____

    _____

4. How did Keith Kokal's experience at the auto parts store help him identify other opportunities?

    _____

    _____

5. What were the underlying beliefs and assumptions that influenced his behavior?

    _____

    _____

Chapter 6: Enthusiastic and somewhat inexperienced

1. While high-growth start-ups, backed by venture capital investors, may require industry experts and a proven top-shelf management team, the reality is that most new ventures are started by inexperienced entrepreneurs with limited knowledge in their field of endeavor. How does the lack of experience enable entrepreneurs to sometimes identify opportunities that those with more experience overlook?

    _____
    _____
    _____

2. How was Carey Mobius able to overcome his lack of experience to transform his family's failing business into a thriving success? What were the skills that enabled him to succeed? What were the underlying beliefs and assumptions that enabled him to succeed?

    _____
    _____
    _____

Chapter 6: Enthusiastic and somewhat inexperienced - Part 2

1. How did Dawn Halfaker overcome her lack of experience when she became an entrepreneur? Why was she able to identify opportunities that others with more experience had overlooked? What were the underlying beliefs and assumptions that enabled her to succeed?

    _____
    _____
    _____

1. Problem solving is the key to every entrepreneur's success. Even those who do develop revolutionary new technologies or complex solutions must apply those solutions to solve real-world problems. David Petite provides a powerful example of a self-taught technology entrepreneur. What were the underlying beliefs and assumptions that encouraged him to become an inventor and entrepreneur?

   _____
   _____
   _____

2. What problem did he identify as his first opportunity as an inventor/entrepreneur?

   _____
   _____

3. How did he know he had a good idea? What obstacles did he face? How did he learn how to develop the technology for his solution?

   _____
   _____

4. What role did luck play in his success with his first invention? How did his first success lead to other opportunities?

   _____
   _____

Chapter 8: Fatal assumptions

1. There are a number of fatal assumptions that often lead aspiring entrepreneurs astray. How are technical knowledge and abilities different from those of an entrepreneur?

   _____
   _____

2. Why do those who possess technical knowledge and abilities often fail as entrepreneurs?

_____

_____

3. How do entrepreneurs minimize their risks? Do they bet everything on a hunch?

_____

_____

4. Explain the difference between small experiments and big bets. What are the underlying assumptions of each?

_____

_____

5. Why is it important to identify a problem first, then to provide a solution? Why is objectivity important to an entrepreneur? How is this concept different from what you previously imagined?

_____

_____

6. What is an "inside-out" perspective? Describe the underlying beliefs and assumptions of an "inside-out" perspective.

_____

_____

7. How does an "inside-out" perspective blind us to opportunities? How does the coffee shop example demonstrate an "inside-out" approach?

_____

_____

8. Describe an "outside-in" approach. How is the "outside-in" approach different from an "inside-out"?

_____

_____

9. Should we expect a good idea to lead to easy success? Why or why not?

_____

_____

10. Which is more important: the idea itself or your abilities as an entrepreneur? Why?

_____

_____

Final Lesson 2 Discussion
How does this concept answer the guiding questions?

1. How do entrepreneurs with limited resources identify and pursue opportunities?
2. How do those who have nothing, create something?

Lesson 2: Recognizing Opportunities - Discussion Notes

_____

_____

_____

_____

_____

Lesson 2: Recognizing Opportunities - Discussion Notes

_____

_____

_____

_____

_____

_____

_____

_____

_____

_____

_____

_____

Lesson 2: Recognizing Opportunities - Discussion Notes

_____

_____

_____

_____

_____

_____

_____

_____

_____

_____

_____

_____

_____

Lesson 2: Recognizing Opportunities - Reflection and Response

Problems are often opportunities in disguise. Entrepreneurs are problem solvers and the secret to their success lies in their ability to identify problems and find solutions.

Reflection:
Do you know of a problem that needs to be solved? When you encounter a problem, do you tend to think about possible solutions? Do you know of a product or service that could be improved? What problems have you encountered that you might be able to solve?

_____

_____

_____

_____

_____

_____

_____

_____

_____

Name: _____ **Date:** _____

Response:
What was the most important aspect of this lesson for you? How can you apply this knowledge in a way that will move you closer to your goals?

_____

_____

_____

_____

_____

_____

_____

_____

_____

_____

_____

Lesson 2: Recognizing Opportunities - Application Assignments

Problems are often opportunities in disguise. Entrepreneurs are problem solvers and the secret to their success lies in their ability to identify problems and find solutions.

Break into groups/teams. Some students may prefer to work alone. Those who may not have an idea can team up with those who do. Note: When forming groups, students should consider teaming up with those who have complementary rather than overlapping skills.

- What's your big idea? Do you have a specific idea for a business? Discuss problems as potential opportunities. Discuss your concept with others in your group. Each group must select a single concept. What problem does this concept solve? What evidence do you have? How many people have this problem? What other solutions are available and how is yours different?

- Determine what you already know about the problem you intend to solve. (Remember the differences between an assumption, a belief and a fact.) Determine the knowledge you need that will help you prove (or disprove) your concept. Remember, it is important to be objective. The next step is to identify possible sources of knowledge.

- Using the Ice House Opportunity Discovery Canvas, document your idea as well as your assumptions about how you might transform that idea into an entrepreneurial opportunity. Share your Opportunity Discovery Canvas as a classroom presentation. Briefly describe what you now know, what your assumptions are and the knowledge you need to help prove or disprove your concept.

Read **Chapter 3: Action** in *Who Owns the Ice House?*

Name: _____ **Date:** _____

ICE HOUSE OPPORTUNITY DISCOVERY CANVAS

Describe the problem being solved or need being fulfilled	**Describe your idea for a product or service**	**Describe solutions currently available**
How is your product or service different?	**How many people have this problem?**	**How will you reach potential customers?** (marketing & sales)
Why will your customers buy your product or service? (What is your brand?)	**How will your customers buy your product or service?** (Online, through partnerships with existing business, standalone store)	**How can you test these assumptions in the real world?** (quickly and cheaply)

Lesson 3: Ideas Into Action

Uncle Cleve's Message

Uncle Cleve was a man of action. He was always in motion and his mind was always fully engaged. Once he had identified an opportunity and gathered the information he needed, he set his plan into motion. He was not one to make excuses and he was not afraid to try something new. Although he had no formal education, he was not afraid to learn. He acted on his ideas and gave little credence to what others thought of him. He focused his precious time and energy on things he could change and work was not his enemy. Rather than approaching work as an unpleasant experience, it was something he took pride in; something he enjoyed. In spite of the circumstances that surrounded him and the limitations that were beyond his control, he chose to focus on those things that he could change. He understood the power of his actions and fully embraced the qualities of the entrepreneurial mindset.

Lesson 3: Ideas Into Action

Overview

Think big. Start small. Act fast. Entrepreneurs are action oriented and they tend to focus their time and energy on things they can change rather than things they cannot. Using case studies, participants learn how entrepreneurs overcome self-imposed limitations and put their ideas into action.

1. Barriers to entry
In chapter one, we'll define the barriers that prevent us from acting on our ideas.

2. Lack of money
In chapter two, we'll discuss the lack of money as an obstacle that can be overcome.

3. Bootstrapping
In chapter three, we'll explore the concept of bootstrapping. We'll learn how entrepreneurs manage to make it work with what they've got by "bootstrapping" their way into business.

4. Proof of concept
In chapter four, we will discuss the importance of "proving your concept". We'll see how entrepreneurs with limited resources "prove their concepts" with real customers.

5. Lack of time
In chapter five, we'll explore the lack of time as an obstacle that entrepreneurs learn to overcome.

6. Lack of experience
In chapter six, we'll discuss the lack of experience as a barrier and how every entrepreneur must learn to overcome it.

7. Fear
In chapter seven, we'll identify fear and self-doubt as a barrier that many entrepreneurs learn to overcome.

8. Re-inventing work In chapter eight, we'll examine the motivation and the perspective that drives entrepreneurs to succeed.

Lesson 3: Ideas Into Action - Chalkboard Notes

_____

_____

_____

_____

_____

_____

_____

_____

_____

_____

Lesson 3: Ideas Into Action - Chalkboard Notes

_____

_____

_____

_____

_____

_____

_____

_____

_____

_____

_____

_____

Name: _____ Date: _____

Lesson 3: Ideas Into Action - Review

True or False - circle one

Chapter 1: Barriers to entry

1. Barriers to entry are the hindrances or obstacles that prevent us from entering a specific business. **T or F**

Chapter 2: Lack of money

2. Most new businesses require bank financing or venture capital investors. **T or F**

Chapter 3: Bootstrapping

3. Entrepreneurs often overcome their lack of money by bootstrapping their way into business. **T or F**

4. Bootstrapping entrepreneurs often buy luxury items to create the appearance of success. **T or F**

5. In many cases, the lack of resources can actually work to an entrepreneur's advantage. **T or F**

Chapter 4: Proof of Concept

6. The term "proof of concept" refers to an entrepreneur's ability to convince others that they have a good idea. **T or F**

7. Ted and Sirena Moore obtained a bank loan to start their construction cleaning business. **T or F**

Chapter 5: Lack of time

8. Starting a business should only be attempted by those who are unemployed or not enrolled in school. **T or F**

Chapter 6: Lack of experience

9. Most successful entrepreneurs have years of experience in their industry before starting a business of their own. **T or F**

Chapter 7: Fear

10. Fear is an "internal barrier" that stops many would-be entrepreneurs from acting on their ideas. **T or F**

11. We often attribute the success of others to an innate gift, a rare personality or luck - things that are beyond our control. **T or F**

Chapter 7: Fear - Part 2

12. According to author Carol Dweck, those with a fixed mindset believe their basic qualities, like their intelligence or talent, are simply fixed traits. **T or F**

13. Entrepreneurs must learn to develop a growth mindset. **T or F**

Chapter 7: Fear - Part 3

14. As an aspiring entrepreneur, it is best to limit our activities and stick to what we know. **T or F**

Chapter 8: Re-inventing work

15. Entrepreneurs are intrinsically motivated. **T or F**

Lesson 3: Ideas Into Action - Discussions

Chapter 1: Barriers to entry

1. What do you think are the greatest barriers to entry for becoming an entrepreneur?

   _____

   _____

2. Are they internal or external barriers?

   _____

   _____

Chapter 2: Lack of money

1. Do you think that it "takes money to make money"? Why or why not?

   _____

   _____

2. Do you know of an entrepreneur who started a business with little or no money? How did they overcome their lack of money?

   _____

   _____

3. How did Ryan Blair characterize the lack of money as an obstacle to starting a business?

   _____

   _____

4. What is the difference between an obstacle and a priority?

   _____

   _____

1. Describe the term bootstrapping and why it is important to an entrepreneur.

   _____

   _____

2. How can the lack of resources become an advantage to an entrepreneur?

   _____

   _____

3. How did Ted and Sirena Moore bootstrap their business? What resources did they have? What challenges did they face? What sacrifices did they make? How did they overcome their lack of money?

   _____

   _____

4. Why didn't they pursue investment or a loan?

   _____

   _____

5. What were the underlying beliefs and assumptions that influenced their behavior?

   _____

   _____

6. What were Ted's strengths? What were his weaknesses?

   _____

   _____

7. What were Sirena's strengths? What were her weaknesses?

   _____

   _____

8. How did they spend the money they earned?

_____

_____

Chapter 4: Proof of Concept

1. Describe the term "proof of concept".

_____

_____

2. How did Ted and Sirena prove their concept?

_____

_____

3. Why is it important to acknowledge the uncertainty of a new venture?

_____

_____

4. How does proving your concept empower you as an entrepreneur?

_____

_____

5. How does it help reduce risk?

_____

_____

6. How can proving your concept increase your chances of finding money you need to start your business?

_____

_____

7. How did Ted and Sirena find their first customers?

_____

_____

8. How do customers determine the validity of our ideas?

_____

_____

Chapter 5: Lack of time

1. Time is the currency we all have. How do entrepreneurs overcome the lack of time as a barrier? What sacrifices must you make?

_____

_____

2. In terms of time, what sacrifices did Palwasha Siddiqi make to become an entrepreneur?

_____

_____

3. How did Keith Kokal manage his time as well as the risks involved in starting his business?

_____

_____

4. How did they spend or invest their time?

_____

_____

5. How did luck play a role in their success? How did their choices play a role?

_____

_____

6. What were the underlying beliefs and assumptions that drove their behavior?

_____

_____

7. Do you think it is necessary to quit your job or drop out of school to become an entrepreneur? What alternatives do you see?

_____

_____

Chapter 6: Lack of experience

1. How do entrepreneurs like Ted and Sirena Moore, Brian Scudamore, Dawn Halfaker or Carey Mobius overcome their lack of experience as aspiring entrepreneurs?

_____

_____

2. Describe an example of something you started without experience. Describe the stages of learning you experienced as you became more competent along the way. How confident were you at the beginning? How did your confidence grow over time? Did you make mistakes? What did you learn from them?

_____

_____

3. As an entrepreneur, how can you manage your risk when you don't have experience?

_____

_____

Chapter 7: Fear

1. Fear is an invisible barrier - *a self-imposed limitation that prevents many from achieving their true potential.* Describe the similarities and differences between our beliefs and an invisible barrier.

_____

_____

2. Describe an example of how fear may prevent you from taking action.

_____

_____

3. Describe an experience when you deliberately pushed yourself beyond your comfort zone.

_____

_____

4. In some cases, we make excuses rather than acknowledge our fears. How does the "good" become the enemy of the "great"?

_____

_____

Chapter 7: Fear - Part 2

1. How did Jason Campbell describe his experience of overcoming his fear?

_____

_____

2. How did his entrepreneurial experience influence his beliefs in his own abilities?

_____

_____

3. Do successful entrepreneurs have fear?

_____

_____

4. How did Susana Cabrera manage her fears?

_____

_____

5. How did she demonstrate her power to choose? Was she operating from an internal or an external locus of control? How?

_____

_____

6. What was the result of overcoming her fear? How did her beliefs change as the result of her actions?

_____

_____

Chapter 7: Fear - Part 3

1. What was the most important thing you learned from the entrepreneurs featured in this chapter?

_____

_____

2. How has fear or the lack of confidence prevented you from doing something you wanted to do? Did you make excuses or did you acknowledge your fear? Did you overcome your lack of confidence? If so, how? Why is it important to acknowledge your fear rather than make excuses?

_____

_____

Chapter 8: Re-inventing work

1. What influenced David Petite to become an entrepreneur?

_____

_____

2. How did he approach his work differently than most? What motivated him to work 42 hours straight?

_____

_____

3. Do you think this motivation is something he was born with or do you think it is the result of his underlying beliefs and assumptions?

_____

_____

4. Describe the specific beliefs and assumptions that motivate entrepreneurs to work long and hard to accomplish their goals.

_____

_____

Chapter 8: Re-inventing work - Part 2

1. Was David Petite motivated by money (extrinsic) or by the enjoyment of the work itself (intrinsic) - by his ability to solve problems and make a difference in the lives of others?

_____

_____

2. Describe the difference between a fixed and a growth mindset. Provide an example of each.

_____

_____

3. How did Brian Scudamore describe his motivation to succeed?

_____

_____

4. How did Susana Cabrera describe her work?

_____

_____

How does this concept answer the guiding questions?

1. How do entrepreneurs with limited resources identify and pursue opportunities?
2. How do those who have nothing, create something?

Lesson 3: Ideas Into Action - Discussion Notes

_____

_____

_____

_____

_____

_____

_____

_____

_____

Lesson 3: Ideas Into Action - Discussion Notes

Name: _____ Date: _____

Lesson 3: Ideas Into Action - Reflection and Response

Think big. Start small. Act fast. Entrepreneurs are action oriented and they tend to focus their time and energy on things they can change rather than things they cannot.

Reflection:
What is preventing you from taking the steps necessary to accomplish your goals? Are the barriers external, such as lack of knowledge and resources, time and money? Or are they internal barriers such as complacency, fear or a lack of confidence?

_____

_____

_____

_____

_____

_____

_____

_____

Name: _____ **Date:** _____

What was the most important aspect of this lesson for you? How will it change your behavior in a way that will move you closer to your goals? What will you have to give up in order to accomplish your goals?

_____

_____

_____

_____

_____

_____

_____

_____

_____

_____

_____

Lesson 3: Ideas Into Action - Application Assignments

Think big. Start small. Act fast. Entrepreneurs are action oriented and they tend to focus their time and energy on things they can change rather than things they cannot.

OK. Now it's time to put your ideas into action. Now that you have identified possible sources of knowledge, it's time to determine what actions are required and who will be responsible for carrying out specific actions. In other words, it's time to get out of the classroom and test your ideas in the real world. Here are some suggestions:

- Conduct an ad-hoc survey. Speak to several people who may have the same problem. (Those who may be potential customers). Ask them if your solution makes sense to them. Why or why not? Ask them what suggestions they might have. If possible, present them with a sample (prototype) of your proposed solution.

- Speak to an entrepreneur or business owner who may have experience in the same or similar field. Ask them what they think about your idea and ask them for suggestions. You might also ask them if they would be willing to speak to your class about their experience and journey to becoming an entrepreneur.

- Speak to successful business owners or other community leaders. Ask them if they have any advice for you regarding the problem you are trying to solve. Ask them if they can suggest someone else who be able to provide insight.

- Revise your Opportunity Discovery Canvas. Describe the actions you took, who you spoke to, what you observed and, most importantly, what you've learned.

Read **Chapter 4: Knowledge** in *Who Owns the Ice House?*

Name: _____ Date: _____

ICE HOUSE OPPORTUNITY DISCOVERY CANVAS

Describe the problem being solved or need being fulfilled

Describe your idea for a product or service

Describe solutions currently available

How is your product or service different?

How many people have this problem?

How will you reach potential customers?
(marketing & sales)

Why will your customers buy your product or service?
(What is your brand?)

How will your customers buy your product or service?
(Online, through partnerships with existing business, standalone store)

How can you test these assumptions in the real world?
(quickly and cheaply)

Lesson 4: Pursuit of Knowledge

Uncle Cleve's Message

Although Uncle Cleve had little formal education, he was a wise man who understood the value of knowledge and was not afraid to learn. He was a curious man and he understood the power of knowledge and the clear connection between knowledge, effort and reward. He developed an insatiable curiosity about the world around him, and for Uncle Cleve, learning became a self-directed, lifelong pursuit. Rather than accepting his lack of formal education as a limitation, he sought knowledge wherever he could find it. Rather than spend his idle time carelessly, he constantly searched for answers, his mind perpetually engaged. An avid reader, he sought knowledge and insight from others. He was an observant man who became a lifelong student as well as a teacher. He was also open-minded, willing to challenge his own assumptions, as well as the commonly held beliefs of those around him.

Lesson 4: Pursuit of Knowledge

Overview

Our effort can only take us as far as our understanding. Entrepreneurs are self-directed, life-long learners who understand the power of knowledge combined with effort. Participants learn how entrepreneurs find the knowledge they need, combining traditional classroom learning with interaction and observation, experimentation and adaptation.

1. The power of knowledge
In chapter one, we will explore the power of knowledge combined with effort.

2. Learning defined
In chapter two, we'll define formal learning and examine its relevance to an entrepreneur.

3. The "aha" moment
In chapter three, we'll describe the "aha" moment that awakens our curiosity and ignites an innate desire to learn.

4. Planning for success
In chapter four, we'll discuss the importance of planning. We'll see how entrepreneurs learn by doing, often taking a ready, fire, aim approach.

5. A word of caution
In chapter five, a word of caution: we'll discuss the importance of approaching our ideas as unproven assumptions rather than established facts.

6. Knowledge as a barrier
In chapter six, we'll look at the learning curve and discuss knowledge as a barrier that stops many in their tracks.

7. Learning redefined
In chapter seven, we'll describe the process of informal learning. We'll see how entrepreneurs learn to find the knowledge they need to get where they want to go.

Lesson 4: Pursuit of Knowledge - Chalkboard Notes

_____

_____

_____

_____

_____

_____

_____

_____

_____

_____

_____

_____

Lesson 4: Pursuit of Knowledge - Chalkboard Notes

_____

_____

_____

_____

_____

_____

_____

_____

_____

_____

_____

_____

_____

Name: _____ Date: _____

Lesson 4: Pursuit of Knowledge - Review

True or False - circle one

Chapter 1: The power of knowledge

1. Knowledge alone is the engine that drives an entrepreneur.   **T or F**

2. Entrepreneurs are born with a unique sense of curiosity.   **T or F**

Chapter 2: Learning defined

3. Entrepreneurship often discourages students from pursuing a formal education.   **T or F**

Chapter 2: Learning defined - Part 2

4. An entrepreneurial experience provides a new perspective and fosters a desire to learn.   **T or F**

Chapter 4: Planning for success

5. Careful planning is the key to every entrepreneur's success.   **T or F**

Chapter 4: Planning for success - Part 2

6. Too much planning can blind us to unforeseen opportunities.   **T or F**

Chapter 5: A word of caution

7. A belief is a known fact.   **T or F**

8. As an aspiring entrepreneur, it is important to trust our beliefs as if they were facts.   **T or F**

Chapter 6: Knowledge as a barrier

9. Learning is a challenge for many aspiring entrepreneurs.   **T or F**

Chapter 7: Learning redefined

10. Informal learning can only take place within a structured learning environment.
    T or F

11. Informal learning often becomes a life-long process for an entrepreneur.
    T or F

12. Entrepreneurs often combine formal and informal learning.   **T or F**

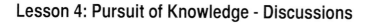

Lesson 4: Pursuit of Knowledge - Discussions

Chapter 1: The power of knowledge

1. As we have said, doing what we have always done will likely get us what
   we have always gotten. How does knowledge influence our choices?

   _____

   _____

2. Why is a growth mindset important to an entrepreneurial mindset and the
   pursuit of knowledge?

   _____

   _____

3. Are entrepreneurs born with an unusual sense of curiosity?

   _____

   _____

4. How does their mindset influence their behavior when it comes to
   curiosity and the pursuit of knowledge?

   _____

   _____

5. How can the combination of knowledge and effort empower an
   entrepreneur to succeed?

   _____

   _____

1. What is the difference between formal and informal learning? Which do you prefer and why?

   _____

   _____

2. How did Ryan Blair's actions as a young man reinforce his beliefs? How did entrepreneurship influence his approach to learning?

   _____

   _____

3. How did Rodney Walker's actions as a young man reinforce his beliefs?

   _____

   _____

4. How did entrepreneurship influence his approach to learning? How did his perception of his abilities change?

   _____

   _____

Chapter 2: Learning defined - Part 2

1. How did Jason Campbell's perspective towards learning change over time?

   _____

   _____

2. What subjects do you enjoy the most? What has been your motivation to learn?

   _____

   _____

Chapter 3: The "aha" moment

1. How does entrepreneurship influence our ability and our willingness to learn?

   _____

   _____

2. What subjects spark your interest and your willingness to learn? Why?

   _____

   _____

3. Describe an entrepreneur's incentive to learn.

   _____

   _____

Chapter 4: Planning for success

1. Why is it important to plan?

   _____

   _____

2. How can too much planning lead us astray?

   _____

   _____

3. How can the lack of planning lead us astray?

   _____

   _____

4. How do entrepreneurs balance planning with action without taking unnecessary risks?

   _____

   _____

5. How do they use face-to-face selling as ad-hoc market research?

_____

_____

6. How did Susana Cabrera approach market research? How did it affect her confidence? What role did luck play? What about choice?

_____

_____

7. How did Dawn Halfaker plan for her business? How did she learn?

_____

_____

8. What were the underlying beliefs and assumptions that drove her behavior?

_____

_____

9. At which stage did she plan her business? (Before she started or after she had begun?)

_____

_____

Chapter 4: Planning for success - Part 2

1. What lesson did David Petite learn from his first business failure? What could he and his partner have done differently to avoid their mistake?

_____

_____

2. What opportunities did Brian Scudamore discover once he had started his business?

_____

_____

3. How would careful planning have increased his ability to succeed? How could it have hindered him or discouraged him from starting?

_____

_____

4. What was he risking at the start? How did he learn through interaction and observation, experimentation and adaptation?

_____

_____

Chapter 5: A word of caution

1. What is the difference between a belief and a fact? How does an assumption differ from a belief?

_____

_____

2. Why is it important for entrepreneurs to approach their ideas as unproven assumptions rather than facts? Describe an example.

_____

_____

3. How does the process of experimentation help entrepreneurs minimize their risks?

_____

_____

Chapter 6: Knowledge as a barrier

1. How does the lack of knowledge prevent some from achieving their goals?

_____

_____

2. What example did Ted Moore describe? What did he describe as the solution? What did Sirena describe as the mindset that will enable you to overcome this obstacle?

_____

_____

3. How did Palwasha describe her experience when she first arrived in the US? How did she overcome her fear?

_____

_____

Chapter 7: Learning redefined

1. How did Sirena Moore take an entrepreneurial approach to learning?

_____

_____

2. How did she learn to conduct herself as a business professional? How did she learn how successful entrepreneurs handle their wealth?

_____

_____

3. What were the underlying beliefs and assumptions that empowered Sirena's desire to learn? What was her motivation to learn?

_____

_____

4. How did Keith Kokal approach learning as an entrepreneur? What was his motivation to learn? (intrinsic or extrinsic?)

_____

_____

5. How did Lydia Gutierrez learn to be an entrepreneur? What was her motivation to learn?

_____

_____

6. How did Brian Scudamore learn how to become an entrepreneur?

_____

_____

7. What step did he add to the combination of knowledge and effort? Why is this an important step?

_____

_____

8. Does his approach reflect an internal or external locus of control? How did Brian describe his view of an internal locus of control?

_____

_____

9. How did he overcome his learning disorder? What specific things does he do to learn? How did he define an MBA?

_____

_____

10. How did David Petite learn to become a successful entrepreneur?

_____

_____

11. How does the mindset of these entrepreneurs differ from others when it comes to learning?

_____

_____

12. Describe the difference between an intrinsic and an extrinsic motivation to learn.

_____

_____

Final Lesson 4 Discussion
How does this concept answer the guiding questions?

1. How do entrepreneurs with limited resources identify and pursue opportunities?
2. How do those who have nothing, create something?

Lesson 4: Pursuit of Knowledge - Discussion Notes

_____

_____

_____

_____

_____

_____

_____

_____

Lesson 4: Pursuit of Knowledge - Discussion Notes

_____

_____

_____

_____

_____

_____

_____

_____

_____

_____

_____

_____

Lesson 4: Pursuit of Knowledge - Discussion Notes

_____

_____

_____

_____

_____

_____

_____

_____

_____

_____

_____

_____

Name: _____ Date: _____

Lesson 4: Pursuit of Knowledge - Reflection and Response

Our effort can only take us as far as our understanding. Entrepreneurs are self-directed, life-long learners who understand the power of knowledge combined with effort.

Reflection:
What subjects interest you the most? What is the most effective way for you to learn? If the lack of knowledge is a barrier, how can you acquire the knowledge you need to get where you want to go?

_____

_____

_____

_____

_____

_____

_____

_____

_____

_____

Name: _____ Date: _____

Response:
What was the most important aspect of this lesson for you? How will it change your behavior in a way that will move you closer to your goals?

_____

_____

_____

_____

_____

_____

_____

_____

_____

_____

Lesson 4: Pursuit of Knowledge - Application Assignments

Our effort can only take us as far as our understanding. Entrepreneurs are self-directed, life-long learners who understand the power of knowledge combined with effort.

- Now it's time to reflect on what you have learned and determine how the knowledge you have acquired has altered your perspective. What adjustments need to be made? What additional knowledge is required?

- Identify additional sources of knowledge that will help you answer the questions outlined in the Opportunity Discovery Canvas. Those sources of knowledge can be online resources or your local library as well as experienced entrepreneurs, mentors or other advisers. Potential customers can also provide valuable knowledge and insight during the opportunity discovery process.

- Remember to keep an open mind. Through the Opportunity Discovery process, you may find evidence to support your original idea, however, through the process of interaction and observation, experimentation and adaptation you may also uncover a greater opportunity. You may also find evidence that your idea is not likely to lead to success.

- Use your Opportunity Discovery Canvas to prepare a written explanation or classroom presentation describing what you have learned through this discovery cycle. Briefly describe how the discovery process altered or reinforced your assumptions. Also describe your interactions and observations with entrepreneurs, advisers or potential customers. Describe the single most important thing you have learned thus far.

Read **Chapter 5: Wealth** in *Who Owns the Ice House?*

Name: _____ Date: _____

ICE HOUSE OPPORTUNITY DISCOVERY CANVAS

Describe the problem being solved or need being fulfilled

Describe your idea for a product or service

Describe solutions currently available

How is your product or service different?

How many people have this problem?

How will you reach potential customers?
(marketing & sales)

Why will your customers buy your product or service?
(What is your brand?)

How will your customers buy your product or service?
(Online, through partnerships with existing business, standalone store)

How can you test these assumptions in the real world?
(quickly and cheaply)

Lesson 5: Creating Wealth

Uncle Cleve's Message

Uncle Cleve was internally driven and he understood that his choices and actions rather than his circumstances would ultimately determine the outcome of his life. It was this fundamental shift in his perspective that separated him from others. It was a subtle, yet profound transformation that empowered him to succeed. He spent his time and energy only on things that would improve his life in the long term and lead him toward his goal. His approach to money was no different. Rather than spending his money to buy unnecessary things or to impress others, Uncle Cleve saw money as a tool to invest in his future, a tool that would enable him to create wealth. He was future-focused and willing to make sacrifices to get where he wanted to go. He was willing to live beneath his means because he valued financial freedom (his goal) more than he valued the opinions of others. Temptations surrounded him just as they did others, yet he developed the ability to subordinate an impulse to a higher value—to his goals, his hopes, and his dreams. He did not drive expensive cars nor eat in fancy restaurants. He avoided the credit trap that so many others fell into. His shoes were old and his clothes were worn yet he took money to the bank and his deposits always exceeded his expenses. And while his money accumulated in the bank, his mind was focused on his next opportunity. Rather than being paid by the hour in a job where someone else controlled his future, Uncle Cleve was focused on solving problems and creating value for others and he understood that he could do that by focusing on saving his income. That way, when an opportunity presented itself, he had the resources to take action.

Lesson 5: Creating Wealth

Overview

Spending or investing? For most, it's not the lack of money that prevents us from prospering. In this lesson, we will learn fundamental concepts of financial literacy from an entrepreneurial perspective. Lastly, we will uncover how entrepreneurs manage their expenses, handle credit and leverage their abilities to create sustainable wealth.

1. Wealth perceived
In chapter one, we'll examine some of the common misconceptions about wealth as well as the underlying beliefs and assumptions that so often lead us astray.

2. Wealth defined
In chapter two, we'll define the four basic concepts that become the foundation for creating wealth.

3. Spending vs. investing
In chapter three, we'll explore the fundamental difference between spending and investing when it comes to creating wealth.

4. The credit trap
In chapter four, we'll learn how to use credit as leverage to advance our goals rather than a burden that keeps us stuck.

5. An entrepreneur's approach
In chapter five, we'll examine an entrepreneur's approach. We'll see how entrepreneurs like Uncle Cleve create sustainable wealth regardless of the circumstances from which they begin.

Lesson 5: Creating Wealth - Chalkboard Notes

_____

_____

_____

_____

_____

_____

_____

_____

_____

_____

_____

_____

Lesson 5: Creating Wealth - Chalkboard Notes

_____

_____

_____

_____

_____

_____

_____

_____

_____

_____

_____

_____

Name: _____ Date: _____

Lesson 5: Creating Wealth - Review

True or False - circle one

Chapter 1: Wealth perceived

1. The appearance of wealth is usually a good indication of a person's true wealth. **T or F**

2. Most people who accumulate wealth have done so through luck or inheritance. **T or F**

3. Those who do have wealth are not likely to display it. **T or F**

Chapter 1: Wealth perceived - Part 2

4. The motivation to become wealthy is different from the motivation to appear wealthy. **T or F**

Chapter 2: Wealth defined

5. The term income refers to money that "comes in" to a household or a business. **T or F**

6. An expense is the money that is spent on living expenditures or to operate a business. **T or F**

7. Discretionary income is the total amount of money a person earns. **T or F**

8. An income statement enables you to keep track of how much you earn. **T or F**

9. The term asset refers to something you own that has monetary value. **T or F**

10. The term liability refers to a major purchase. **T or F**

11. The term equity refers to a person's stature among his or her peers. **T or F**

12. A balance sheet provides a snapshot of a person's true wealth. **T or F**

Chapter 2: Wealth defined - Part 2

13. A person with a moderate income may have more wealth than a person with a high income. **T or F**

Chapter 3: Spending vs. investing

14. The terms "spending" and "investing" are synonymous to an entrepreneur.
T or F

Chapter 4: The credit trap

15. Buying things on credit should be avoided at all costs. **T or F**

Chapter 5: An entrepreneur's approach

16. Entrepreneurs like Uncle Cleve create wealth by simply saving every penny they earn. **T or F**

17. As an entrepreneur, our income is limited by the number of hours in a day.
T or F

18. The lack of money prevents most of us from prospering. **T or F**

Lesson 5: Creating Wealth - Discussions

Chapter 1: Wealth perceived

1. What does it mean to be wealthy?

    _____

    _____

    _____

Chapter 1: Wealth perceived - Part 2

1. Describe the difference between those who appear wealthy and those
    who possess true wealth.

    _____

    _____

    _____

2. Describe the underlying motivation for each. Describe the beliefs and
    assumptions that influence the behavior of each.

    _____

    _____

    _____

3. How is our desire to appear wealthy at odds with our ability to create
    wealth?

    _____

    _____

    _____

1. Define the term income. Define the term expense.

   _____
   _____
   _____

2. What is an income statement and what is it used for?

   _____
   _____
   _____

3. What is a balance sheet and what is it used for?

   _____
   _____
   _____

4. What is an asset? Provide an example of an asset.

   _____
   _____
   _____

5. What is a liability? Describe an example of a liability.

   _____
   _____
   _____

6. What is discretionary income and why is it important to an entrepreneur?

   _____
   _____
   _____

1. How can a person with modest income be in a greater position to create wealth than a person with a high income?

    _____
    _____
    _____

2. What role does luck play in the creation of wealth?

    _____
    _____
    _____

Chapter 3: Spending vs. investing

1. Describe the difference between spending and investing. Why is this important to an entrepreneur?

    _____
    _____
    _____

2. How does this concept apply to our use of time?

    _____
    _____
    _____

3. How does this concept empower entrepreneurs?

    _____
    _____
    _____

4. What lesson did Palwasha learn from her mother while living in a refugee camp?

_____

_____

_____

5. How did Payoff.com founder, Scott Saunders, describe the difference between spending and investing?

_____

_____

_____

6. Describe the difference between those who are driven by impulse and those who are driven by their vision, purpose or goal.

_____

_____

_____

7. How does the awareness of choices impact each?

_____

_____

_____

Chapter 4: The credit trap

1. We know that we are often unaware of our mindset and the profound effect it has on our behavior. If we are unaware of our motivation and the mindset that drives our behavior, we are bound to make decisions that lead us astray. What drives your motivation to spend?

_____

_____

_____

2. How does that lack of awareness get us into trouble when it comes to spending?

_____

_____

_____

3. How does the awareness of choices impact our decisions when it comes to using credit?

_____

_____

_____

Chapter 5: An entrepreneur's approach

1. Entrepreneurs like Uncle Cleve learn to live beneath their means yet they focus their time, attention and money on things that are conducive to creating wealth. How does this differ from your previous perception of how wealth is created?

_____

_____

_____

2. What is the motivation to appear wealthy?

_____

_____

_____

3. What is the motivation to create wealth?

_____

_____

_____

4. How does our mindset affect our ability to create wealth?

_____

_____

_____

How does this concept answer the guiding questions?

1. How do entrepreneurs with limited resources identify and pursue opportunities?
2. How do those who have nothing, create something?

Lesson 5: Creating Wealth - Discussion Notes

_____

_____

_____

_____

_____

_____

_____

Lesson 5: Creating Wealth - Discussion Notes

_____

_____

_____

_____

_____

_____

_____

_____

_____

_____

_____

_____

_____

_____

121

Lesson 5: Creating Wealth - Discussion Notes

_____

_____

_____

_____

_____

_____

_____

_____

_____

_____

_____

_____

_____

Name: _____ Date: _____

Lesson 5: Creating Wealth - Reflection and Response

Spending or investing? For most, it's not the lack of money that prevents us from prospering. Entrepreneurs learn to manage their expenses, handle credit and leverage their abilities to create sustainable wealth, regardless of where they start.

Reflection:
Is the ability to create wealth important to you? Why or why not? How do your beliefs affect your ability to create wealth? Do you have the ability to create wealth? What is the greatest barrier that stands in your way?

_____

_____

_____

_____

_____

_____

_____

_____

_____

_____

Name: _____ **Date:** _____

Response:
What was the most important aspect of this lesson for you? How will it change your behavior in a way that will move you closer to your goals?

_____

_____

_____

_____

_____

_____

_____

_____

_____

_____

_____

Lesson 5: Creating Wealth - Application Assignments

Spending or investing? For most, it's not the lack of money that prevents us from prospering. Entrepreneurs learn to manage their expenses, handle credit and leverage their abilities to create sustainable wealth, regardless of where they start.

What resources do you currently have? What resources will you need? Where can you find the resources you need?

In the previous assignments, we have addressed the importance of action combined with knowledge as the engine that drives an entrepreneur. The purpose of this assignment is to determine the resources you have, as well as the resources you will need to get started. Remember that, in addition to money, resources can include time, knowledge, tools and people.

- How have other entrepreneurs overcome the lack of money to start their business?

- How can you overcome the lack of money to start your business?

- Identify the resources you currently have.

- How will you invest your time and money so that you can accomplish your goals?

Prepare a brief written explanation or classroom presentation describing the resources you currently have, the resources you will need and how you plan to find the resources you need to accomplish your goals. Briefly describe how you can "bootstrap" your business using the resources you currently have.

Read **Chapter 6: Brand** in *Who Owns the Ice House?*

Name: _____   Date: _____

ICE HOUSE OPPORTUNITY DISCOVERY CANVAS

Describe the problem being solved or need being fulfilled

Describe your idea for a product or service

Describe solutions currently available

How is your product or service different?

How many people have this problem?

How will you reach potential customers?
(marketing & sales)

Why will your customers buy your product or service?
(What is your brand?)

How will your customers buy your product or service?
(Online, through partnerships with existing business, standalone store)

How can you test these assumptions in the real world?
(quickly and cheaply)

Lesson 6: Building Your Brand

Uncle Cleve's Message

Uncle Cleve understood that problems were opportunities. He knew that if he could solve problems for other people, he could also empower himself. He also understood the power of being reliable and that his reputation was an essential aspect of his ability to succeed. He also comprehended that it was an aspect of his life that he could control. Central to Uncle Cleve's success as an entrepreneur was the simple fact that he was reliable. The people in Glen Allan, Mississippi knew they could count on him. They trusted him to solve their problems. They knew his word was his bond. They knew he neither gave nor accepted excuses. They knew they could set their clocks to Uncle Cleve. Uncle Cleve had no patents to protect his ideas. His word was his "intellectual property." Reliability was his brand. It was the promise he made to his customers. The more people who knew that they could count on Cleve, the more opportunities he found. They not only trusted him to deliver ice, they also bought wood and coal from him in the winter and they allowed him to repair their high-dollar cars. It was his commitment to his word that gave him confidence. It put the lift in his stride and the twinkle in his eye. Uncle Cleve was inner directed, and his reputation was something he could control. Although it would have been easy for him to do otherwise, Uncle Cleve did not discriminate. He treated everyone fairly. Even when he faced a situation where humiliation seemed the only outcome, Uncle Cleve managed to maintain his dignity. He refused, taking the high road and refusing to lower himself to someone else's dismal standards. By doing what he said he would do, rain or shine, he watched his business grow.

Lesson 6: Building Your Brand

Overview

Actions speak louder than words. Entrepreneurs are problem solvers and reliability is the key to their success. Using case studies and modern-day examples, we will learn how entrepreneurs transform simple solutions into big opportunities by building a reputation for reliability.

1. Brand defined
In chapter one, we'll define the term brand in a way that is relevant and actionable to an aspiring entrepreneur.

2. Defining your brand
In chapter two, we'll discuss the importance of understanding your customers as the key to defining your brand.

3. Communicating your brand
In chapter three, we'll learn how entrepreneurs communicate their brand through their words as well as their actions. We'll also see how they leverage their brand to overcome inertia and communicate value to potential customers.

4. Building your brand
In chapter four, we'll learn how entrepreneurs build their brand. You'll learn firsthand how they transform simple solutions into a sustainable success by being consistent and reliable.

5. Confidence
In chapter five, we'll examine the role of confidence, where it comes from and why it is important.

Lesson 6: Building Your Brand - Chalkboard Notes

_____

_____

_____

_____

_____

_____

_____

_____

_____

_____

_____

Lesson 6: Building Your Brand - Chalkboard Notes

_____

_____

_____

_____

_____

_____

_____

_____

_____

_____

_____

_____

Name: _____ Date: _____

Lesson 6: Building Your Brand - Review

True or False - circle one

Chapter 1: Brand defined

1. A brand is merely a symbol that enables your customers to identify your business from others. **T or F**

Chapter 1: Brand defined - Part 2

2. As an aspiring entrepreneur, branding can be important to getting your foot in the door. **T or F**

3. As an entrepreneur, a well designed logo or website is more important than being reliable and delivering on your promise. **T or F**

Chapter 2: Defining your brand

4. Defining our brand requires us to understand the problem we are solving from our customer's point of view. **T or F**

5. Inexperienced entrepreneurs often brand by default. **T or F**

Chapter 2: Defining your brand - Part 2

6. If you have a valuable product or service, the packaging is not important. **T or F**

7. Market research begins with two important questions: who is our customer and why would they want to buy? **T or F**

Chapter 3: Communicating your brand

8. As an entrepreneur, there are two distinct means of communication: one is explicit, the other implicit. **T or F**

9. An explicit message is more important than an implicit message. **T or F**

Name: _____ **Date:** _____

Chapter 4: Building your brand

10. Entrepreneurs often conduct market research through face-to-face selling.
    T or F

Chapter 5: Confidence

11. Confidence is something we either have or we don't.   **T or F**

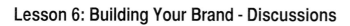

Lesson 6: Building Your Brand - Discussions

Chapter 1: Brand defined

1. Where did the term branding originate and how has it changed?

    _____
    _____
    _____

2. What are the two components of a brand?

    _____
    _____
    _____

Chapter 1: Brand defined - Part 2

1. Why is branding important to an aspiring entrepreneur?

    _____
    _____
    _____

2. How does an entrepreneur develop their brand once they find their first customers?

    _____
    _____
    _____

Chapter 2: Defining your brand

1. Why is it important to understand your customer's point of view?

    _____
    _____
    _____

2. What is the process entrepreneurs undertake to learn about their customers? What methods do they use?

_____

_____

_____

3. Describe the concept of branding by default.

_____

_____

_____

4. What are some of the common pitfalls of branding by default? Describe an example.

_____

_____

_____

5. How did Brian Scudamore use branding to transform a simple idea into a sustainable success?

_____

_____

_____

6. What are the two questions that form the basis of market research?

_____

_____

_____

7. How would you interpret the concept of "seek to understand - then to be understood"?

_____

_____

_____

8. Why is this concept important to defining your brand?

_____

_____

_____

Chapter 3: Communicating your brand

1. Describe an example of an explicit message.

_____

_____

_____

2. Describe an example of nonverbal or implicit communication.

_____

_____

_____

3. Which is more powerful? Why?

_____

_____

_____

4. What message does an old beat-up truck with plywood sides convey?

_____

_____

_____

5. What message does a clean and brightly painted truck with a neatly dressed and courteous driver convey?

_____

_____

_____

135

6. Why is this important to an entrepreneur?

_____

_____

_____

7. How can we convey an explicit message that we can be counted on to deliver on what we say?

_____

_____

_____

8. How can we convey a nonverbal or implicit message that we are competent and that we can be counted on to deliver what we say?

_____

_____

_____

9. Which is more believable? Why?

_____

_____

_____

Chapter 4: Building your brand

1. How did Sirena and her father Ted build their brand?

_____

_____

_____

2. How did Jason Campbell build his brand?

_____

_____

_____

1. What is the most important aspect of your brand? Why?

   _____

   _____

   _____

2. What are some of the underlying beliefs and assumptions required to build a successful brand?

   _____

   _____

   _____

3. How does our ability to choose affect our ability to be reliable and build a successful brand?

   _____

   _____

   _____

Chapter 5: Confidence

1. Where do entrepreneurs get their confidence? Are they born with it or can it be developed over time?

   _____

   _____

   _____

2. What is required to develop confidence?

   _____

   _____

   _____

3. How did Rodney Walker and Palwasha Saddiqi develop their confidence?

    _____

    _____

    _____

4. Why is this important to building your brand?

    _____

    _____

    _____

Final Lesson 6 Discussion
How does this concept answer the guiding questions?

1. How do entrepreneurs with limited resources identify and pursue opportunities?
2. How do those who have nothing, create something?

Lesson 6: Building Your Brand - Discussion Notes

_____

_____

_____

_____

_____

_____

_____

Lesson 6: Building Your Brand - Discussion Notes

_____

_____

_____

_____

_____

_____

_____

_____

_____

_____

_____

_____

_____

Lesson 6: Building Your Brand - Discussion Notes

_____

_____

_____

_____

_____

_____

_____

_____

_____

_____

_____

_____

_____

Lesson 6: Building Your Brand - Reflection and Response

Actions speak louder than words. Entrepreneurs are problem solvers; they learn
how to transform simple solutions into big opportunities where reliability is the key.

Reflection:
What does the term branding mean to you? How can the concept of branding help
you accomplish your goals?

_____

_____

_____

_____

_____

_____

_____

_____

_____

_____

Name: _____ **Date:** _____

Response:
What was the most important aspect of this lesson for you? How will it change your behavior in a way that will move you closer to your goals?

_____

_____

_____

_____

_____

_____

_____

_____

_____

_____

Lesson 6: Building Your Brand - Application Assignments

Actions speak louder than words. Entrepreneurs are problem solvers; they learn how to transform simple solutions into big opportunities where reliability is the key.

What is your brand? Why will people buy from you? How will your customers know they can count on you to do what you say you will do? What message do you want to convey to your customers? How will you communicate your message?

■ Identify a business that has a good reputation. What message do they communicate? How do they communicate that message? How is their message (what they say about themselves) consistent with their reputation (what their customers say about them)?

■ Identify a business that does not have a good reputation. What message do they communicate? How do they communicate their message? How is their message (what they say about themselves) consistent with their reputation (what their customers say about them)?

■ What message would you like to communicate to your customers? How do you intend to communicate your message?

■ How will you invest your time and money so that you can accomplish your goals?

Update your Opportunity Discovery Canvas. Describe your brand; the message you want to communicate to your customers and how you intend to communicate that message. You can provide an example such as a logo, a website, a uniform or a flyer. Provide at least one example of how you will communicate your brand through an explicit message as well as an implicit message.

Read **Chapter 7: Community** in *Who Owns the Ice House?*

Name: _____   Date: _____

ICE HOUSE OPPORTUNITY DISCOVERY CANVAS

Describe the problem being solved or need being fulfilled	Describe your idea for a product or service	Describe solutions currently available

How is your product or service different?	How many people have this problem?	How will you reach potential customers? (marketing & sales)

Why will your customers buy your product or service? (What is your brand?)	How will your customers buy your product or service? (Online, through partnerships with existing business, standalone store)	How can you test these assumptions in the real world? (quickly and cheaply)

Lesson 7: Creating Community

Uncle Cleve's Message

Because he was future focused, Uncle Cleve taught himself to stick with others who were the same. He made the choice to create the life he wanted rather than the life everyone around him had accepted. Uncle Cleve chose to focus his time and attention on things he could change, on the aspects of his life over which he had control. He had little time for the juke joints and neighborhood saloons. He did not engage in gossip and small talk. Instead he earned the respect of others and created a community of respect, a network of action-oriented individuals who shared his commitment to success. He earned the respect of others and he paid attention to what other business owners were doing. Uncle Cleve was a student as well as a teacher. He learned from the success of others and, thankfully, he was willing to pass along what he had learned.

Lesson 7: Creating Community

Overview

Entrepreneurs understand the power of positive influence and they learn to surround themselves with others who have been where they intend to go. In this lesson, we will learn how to tap into a network of entrepreneurs, mentors and trusted advisers within our own communities.

1. Community defined
In chapter one, we'll define a community as a success network of others who have been where we want to go.

2. The value of a network
In chapter two, we'll discuss the value and the influence that a success network can provide.

3. Who is in our network?
In chapter three, we'll examine five separate sources of support from successful entrepreneurs, who have been where we intend to go.

4. Crossing the chasm
In chapter four, we'll describe three distinct phases of transformation and the role our success network plays in each.

5. Building a success network
And finally, in chapter five, we'll discuss how entrepreneurs create their success networks as well as some of the obstacles that often stand in their way.

Lesson 7: Creating Community - Chalkboard Notes

_____

_____

_____

_____

_____

_____

_____

_____

_____

_____

_____

_____

_____

Lesson 7: Creating Community - Chalkboard Notes

_____

_____

_____

_____

_____

_____

_____

_____

_____

_____

_____

_____

_____

Name: _____   Date: _____

Lesson 7: Creating Community - Review

True or False - circle one

Chapter 1: Community defined

1. The need to fit in often keeps us tethered to familiar ways of thinking and acting - tethered to a mindset that often keeps us stuck. **T or F**

2. A social network is a social structure made up of people who are connected by common interests or goals. **T or F**

3. As an entrepreneur, our social network can be described as a success network - a community of entrepreneurs and advisers, mentors and friends who share a common goal and are willing to help us succeed. **T or F**

Chapter 2: The value of a network

4. A success network can become a valuable source of knowledge. **T or F**

Chapter 3: Who is in our network? - Peers - Part 2

5. Peer pressure is a negative influence. **T or F**

Chapter 3: Who is in our network? - Partners

6. As an entrepreneur, partnerships should be avoided at all costs. **T or F**

Chapter 3: Who is in our network? - Professionals

7. Professional service providers such as an attorney or an accountant should also become part of your success network. **T or F**

Chapter 3: Who is in our network? - Employees

8. Creating a strict working environment with clearly defined rules and regulations is the best approach to getting the most out of your employees. **T or F**

Chapter 3: Who is in our network? - Mentors & Advisers

9. The most important members of our success community are mentors and advisers. **T or F**

10. Professional service providers are often the most effective mentors. **T or F**

11. Finding an experienced entrepreneur who is willing to act as a mentor or adviser is a difficult challenge for an aspiring entrepreneur. **T or F**

Chapter 4: Crossing the chasm

12. As an entrepreneur, we will likely undergo a process of personal as well as professional transformation and growth. **T or F**

13. The mindset and the skills that enable us to succeed in one phase of transformation will also enable us to succeed in another. **T or F**

14. Phase one is the entrepreneurial phase of a new business. **T or F**

15. In this critical phase, experienced entrepreneurs can be vital to our success. **T or F**

Chapter 4: Crossing the chasm - Part 2

16. A breakpoint is the point at which a business fails. **T or F**

17. Phase two is characterized by repetition and growth rather than experimentation and adaptation. **T or F**

18. By the time we reach the second phase, we may no longer need a success network to help us grow. **T or F**

19. Many aspiring entrepreneurs fail to acknowledge the experimental or entrepreneurial aspect of phase one. **T or F**

20. While phase two is characterized by management and growth, repetition and improvement, phase three is characterized by complacency and isolation, the assumption of complete knowledge and the refusal to acknowledge change. **T or F**

Lesson 7: Creating Community - Discussions

Chapter 1: Community defined

1. As we have seen, becoming an entrepreneur often requires us to think
    and act in new and different ways. How does becoming an entrepreneur
    differ from a traditional path?

    _____

    _____

    _____

2. A social network is a social structure made up of people who are
    connected by common interests or goals. Do you belong to a social
    network? What are the common interests or goals?

    _____

    _____

    _____

3. Do you know an entrepreneur? How are they different from the others in
    your network of friends or other associates?

    _____

    _____

    _____

Chapter 2: The value of a network

1. A success network can be made up of a variety of people with a wide
    range of interest and abilities. Describe each of the five groups mentioned
    in lesson two. (Peers, partners, professionals, employees, mentors)

    _____

    _____

    _____

2. What type of support can each provide? (Knowledge, network, accountability and support)

_____

_____

Chapter 3: Who is in our network? - Peers

1. As we discussed in lesson one, we all have a tendency to surround ourselves with our peers; those with similar beliefs, ambitions, habits and interests. How do our peers encourage us to continue to think and act as we always have?

_____

_____

_____

2. How do your peers influence your decisions and your behavior?

_____

_____

_____

3. Would your peers be supportive of you becoming an entrepreneur? Would they be able to offer knowledge and experience?

_____

_____

_____

Chapter 3: Who is in our network? - Peers - Part 2

1. The term "peer pressure" is often used in a negative context. Describe an example of positive peer pressure.

_____

_____

_____

2. Which of the entrepreneurs interviewed in this segment were the most interesting to you and why? How did their peers influence their behavior?

_____

_____

_____

Chapter 3: Who is in our network? - Partners

1. What value can a partner provide? What should you look for in a partner?

_____

_____

_____

Chapter 3: Who is in our network? - Employees

1. What value can employees provide? Why is it important to create a positive working environment?

_____

_____

_____

2. Have you ever worked in a 'Type X' environment? Describe the experience, your motivation, level of participation and level of engagement.

_____

_____

_____

3. Have you ever worked in a 'Type Y' environment? How was it different? Describe the experience, your motivation, level of participation and level of engagement.

_____

_____

_____

153

1. Do you currently have a mentor or an adviser? How have they helped you? How did you connect with them? How did they challenge your beliefs? What impact did they have on your life?

    _____
    _____
    _____

Chapter 4: Crossing the chasm

1. Describe the three phases of transformation and why each is important to an entrepreneur.

    _____
    _____
    _____

2. Describe an example of a business in phase one. What value can a success network provide?

    _____
    _____
    _____

Chapter 4: Crossing the chasm - Part 2

1. Describe an example of a business in phase two. What value can a success network provide?

    _____
    _____
    _____

2. Describe an example of a business in phase three. What value can a success network provide?

_____

_____

_____

3. Why is it important to recognize which phase you are in?

_____

_____

_____

4. What did Dr. Land mean by saying "nothing fails like success"?

_____

_____

Chapter 5: Building a success network

1. Why is a success network important to you?

_____

_____

_____

2. What is required to build a success network?

_____

_____

_____

3. How can you connect with other entrepreneurs?

_____

_____

_____

4. How would you go about finding a mentor or an adviser who might be willing to help?

_____

_____

_____

Final Lesson 7 Discussion
How does this concept answer the guiding questions?

1. How do entrepreneurs with limited resources identify and pursue opportunities?
2. How do those who have nothing, create something?

Lesson 7: Creating Community - Discussion Notes

_____

_____

_____

_____

_____

_____

_____

_____

Lesson 7: Creating Community - Discussion Notes

_____

_____

_____

_____

_____

_____

_____

_____

_____

_____

_____

Lesson 7: Creating Community - Discussion Notes

_____

_____

_____

_____

_____

_____

_____

_____

_____

_____

_____

Name: _____   **Date:** _____

Lesson 7: Creating Community - Reflection and Response

Entrepreneurs understand the power of positive influence and they learn to surround themselves with others who have been where they intend to go.

Reflection:
How does your environment and the people around you influence your behavior? Why is it important to develop a success network? Who is in your success network? What type of people do you need to include in your success network? For example, do you need to include peers or advisers, professional service providers, a key employee or a mentor to your success network?

_____

_____

_____

_____

_____

_____

_____

_____

Name: _____ **Date:** _____

_____

_____

_____

_____

_____

_____

_____

_____

_____

_____

_____

Lesson 7: Creating Community - Application Assignments

Entrepreneurs understand the power of positive influence and they learn to surround themselves with others who have been where they intend to go.

Who do you know that might be able to help you accomplish your goals? How can you find people who have been where you want to go that might be willing to help you? Mentoring is a crucial aspect of becoming a successful entrepreneur and surrounding ourselves with success is an important choice.

Who is in your network? Visit a networking or support group in your community that is likely to include other aspiring and accomplished entrepreneurs, small business owners, professional service providers and others who can provide knowledge, guidance and support.

Identify the people you can connect with who may be able to provide knowledge, guidance and support. Ask them about their experience and if they would be willing to share their knowledge and experience.

- **Peers**: Identify a friend or someone you know who is on a similar journey who may provide encouragement, knowledge and support..

- **Partners**: Describe your experience working with partners. (the advantages and disadvantages).

- **Professionals**: Identify a professional, an attorney or an accountant who might be willing to offer guidance and support.

- **Employees**: If you were to hire your first employee, what knowledge and experience would you require?

- **Mentors and advisers**: Identify an experienced entrepreneur in your community who might be willing to act as a mentor or informal adviser.

Prepare a brief classroom presentation describing a person that you (or your group) has identified from each of the five groups. Share something you learned from each of the five. If possible, invite someone from your support group to speak to your class.

Read **Chapter 8: Persistence** in *Who Owns the Ice House?*

Name: _____ Date: _____

ICE HOUSE OPPORTUNITY DISCOVERY CANVAS

Describe the problem being solved or need being fulfilled	Describe your idea for a product or service	Describe solutions currently available

How is your product or service different?	How many people have this problem?	How will you reach potential customers? (marketing & sales)

Why will your customers buy your product or service? (What is your brand?)	How will your customers buy your product or service? (Online, through partnerships with existing business, standalone store)	How can you test these assumptions in the real world? (quickly and cheaply)

Lesson 8: The Power of Persistence

Uncle Cleve's Message

Life was not easy for Uncle Cleve. He worked hard every day. Yet, of all the "secrets" to his success, none is perhaps more powerful than persistence—his refusal to give up. And, like most entrepreneurs, his road to success was not without pitfalls, setbacks, and failures. Yet he knew that he could not fail as long as he refused to quit. While many attribute success to an innate ability, luck, or circumstance, most overlook persistence, a subtle yet powerful mindset that Uncle Cleve surely understood. It is persistence that will enable you to face challenges and overcome obstacles. It is persistence that will empower you to forge ahead in the face of fear and uncertainty and will encourage you to push yourself to find solutions. Like our previous mindset lessons, perseverance is something we can all learn. It does not require specialized knowledge. It does not require a rare ability, an innate talent, or a genius IQ. It does not require access to money, power or privilege. Perseverance and determination are traits we are all capable of. And, more often than not, perseverance is the key to creating success.

Lesson 8: The Power of Persistence

Overview

Entrepreneurship is not about how to "get rich quick" and expecting it to be easy is a mistake. The secret behind every entrepreneur's success is hard work, perseverance and determination. In this lesson, we will learn from experience through several of the Ice House Entrepreneurs, the importance of persistence and the role it plays in every entrepreneur's success story.

1. Dawn Halfaker
   "Focus on what you have"

2. Brian Scudamore
   "Slow and steady wins the race"

3. Ted and Sirena Moore
   "Willing to go the distance"

4. Rodney Walker
   "Imagine something greater"

5. Jason Campbell
   "Adversity is an advantage"

6. Palwasha Saddiqi
   "Nothing is easy"

7. Ryan Blair
   "A poor kid with poor beliefs"

8. David Petite
   "Create your own reality"

Lesson 8: The Power of Persistence - Chalkboard Notes

_____

_____

_____

_____

_____

_____

_____

_____

_____

_____

_____

Lesson 8: The Power of Persistence - Chalkboard Notes

_____

_____

_____

_____

_____

_____

_____

_____

_____

_____

_____

Name: _____ Date: _____

Lesson 8: The Power of Persistence - Review

True or False - circle one

Dawn Halfaker: Focus on what you have

1. Dawn Halfaker always thought of herself as an entrepreneur. **T or F**

2. Dawn's mindset changed when she witnessed another severely disabled veteran who was determined to succeed. **T or F**

Brian Scudamore: Slow and steady wins the race

3. Brian Scudamore's business, 1-800-GOT-JUNK, was an overnight sensation that was successful from the start. **T or F**

4. Brian always knew his junk removal business could reach $100 million in sales. **T or F**

Ted and Sirena Moore: Willing to go the distance

5. Ted Moore learned to develop entrepreneurial skills as a child. **T or F**

6. Ted and his daughter Sirena started their business when they received a six-figure contract. **T or F**

Rodney Walker: Imagine something greater

7. Although he was raised as a foster child, Rodney Walker always knew that somehow he would succeed. **T or F**

8. Rodney's entrepreneurial experience helped him develop an entrepreneurial mindset. **T or F**

Jason Campbell: Adversity is an advantage

9. As an entrepreneur, Jason Campbell discovered that adversity can be an advantage.   **T or F**

10. Jason discovered that once he had the right formula, putting his plan into motion was easy.   **T or F**

Palwasha Siddiqi: Nothing is easy

11. Palwasha Siddiqi faced a number of challenges on the road to becoming an entrepreneur.   **T or F**

12. Palwasha was encouraged by others in her community to become an entrepreneur.   **T or F**

Ryan Blair: A poor kid with poor beliefs

13. Ryan Blair attributed his success to being in the right place at the right time.   **T or F**

14. According to Ryan, success is learned behavior.   **T or F**

David Petite: Create your own reality

15. As a young boy raised by a single mother, David Petite soon learned to rely on others to get where he wanted to go.   **T or F**

16. David discovered that by solving problems for others he could create value for himself.   **T or F**

Lesson 8: The Power of Persistence - Discussions

Dawn Halfaker: Focus on what you have

1. What aspect of Dawn's story inspired you? What motivated her to succeed?

   _____

   _____

   _____

2. Describe some of the underlying assumptions that enabled her to succeed.

   _____

   _____

   _____

3. How did she react to her circumstances? How did she respond? How did she exercise her power to choose? How might others have reacted to her circumstances?

   _____

   _____

   _____

4. Which of the eight life lessons did she demonstrate? How?

   _____

   _____

   _____

5. How did she use her experience and abilities to identify problems and provide solutions?

   _____

   _____

   _____

6. What were her strengths? What were her weaknesses? How did she overcome her weaknesses?

_____

_____

_____

7. How did her story impact your mindset? How do her challenges compare to your own?

_____

_____

_____

8. How will her story encourage your focus on what you have rather than what you don't have?

_____

_____

_____

Brian Scudamore: Slow and steady wins the race

1. What aspect of Brian's story inspired you?

_____

_____

_____

2. What circumstances led him to becoming an entrepreneur? How did he exercise his power to choose?

_____

_____

_____

3. What were his strengths? How did he leverage his strengths?

_____

_____

_____

4. What were his weaknesses? How did he overcome his weaknesses?

_____

_____

_____

5. Which of the eight life lessons did he demonstrate? How?

_____

_____

_____

6. What aspect of his mindset (beliefs and assumptions) enabled him to succeed?

_____

_____

_____

7. How was persistence important to his success? How did his story impact your mindset?

_____

_____

_____

8. Why did he describe his vision as a destination rather than a blueprint?

_____

_____

_____

1. What aspect of Ted and Sirena's story inspired you?

   _____

   _____

   _____

2. How did Ted learn to develop entrepreneurial skills? What was his first entrepreneurial venture?

   _____

   _____

   _____

3. How did Sirena learn to present herself professionally?

   _____

   _____

   _____

4. How did Ted and Sirena complement each other's skills?

   _____

   _____

   _____

5. Which of the eight life lessons did they demonstrate? How?

   _____

   _____

   _____

6. How did Ted demonstrate the power to choose?

   _____

   _____

   _____

7. How did Sirena demonstrate the power to choose?

_____

_____

_____

Ted and Sirena Moore: Willing to go the distance - Part 2

1. How did they build their brand?

_____

_____

_____

2. What were the underlying beliefs and assumptions that empowered them to succeed?

_____

_____

_____

3. What were some of the challenges they faced? How did they overcome those obstacles?

_____

_____

_____

4. How do their challenges compare to your own?

_____

_____

_____

5. How was persistence important to their success?

_____

_____

_____

1. What did you learn from Rodney's story? What aspect of his story inspired you?

    _____

    _____

    _____

2. How did his environment influence his thoughts and his actions?

    _____

    _____

    _____

3. How did his friends influence his thoughts and actions?

    _____

    _____

    _____

4. How did he demonstrate the power to choose?

    _____

    _____

    _____

5. How did Rodney's entrepreneurial experience impact his approach to learning?

    _____

    _____

    _____

6. How did his mindset empower him to succeed?

    _____

    _____

    _____

7. Which of the eight life lessons did he demonstrate? How?

_____

_____

_____

8. How was persistence important to his success?

_____

_____

_____

Jason Campbell: Adversity is an advantage

1. How did Jason's entrepreneurial experience in high school help shift his perspective? How did it influence his locus of control?

_____

_____

_____

2. What challenges did he face? What choices did he make?

_____

_____

_____

3. How did he apply an entrepreneurial mindset to other aspects of his life?

_____

_____

_____

4. How did he use adversity to his advantage?

_____

_____

_____

5. Which of the eight life lessons did he demonstrate? How?

    _____

    _____

    _____

6. How was persistence important to his success?

    _____

    _____

    _____

7. How do his challenges compare to your own?

    _____

    _____

    _____

8. How will his story impact your life?

    _____

    _____

    _____

Palwasha Saddiqi: Nothing is easy

1. What did you like about Palwasha's story? What is the single most
    important lesson we can learn from her experience?

    _____

    _____

    _____

2. What were some of the challenges she faced? How did she overcome
    them?

    _____

    _____

    _____

3. What were the negative influences of her environment? How did she demonstrate the power to choose?

_____

_____

_____

Palwasha Saddiqi: Nothing is easy - Part 2

1. What sacrifices did she make to accomplish her goals? How did luck play a role?

_____

_____

_____

2. Which of the eight life lessons did she demonstrate? How?

_____

_____

_____

3. How was persistence important to her success?

_____

_____

_____

4. How do her challenges compare to your own?

_____

_____

_____

1. How did Ryan's environment influence his behavior as a young man?

   _____

   _____

   _____

2. Where did Ryan get his poor beliefs? How did his beliefs reinforce his behavior?

   _____

   _____

   _____

3. How did he learn how to become an entrepreneur?

   _____

   _____

   _____

4. What events influenced his willingness to change?

   _____

   _____

   _____

5. Which of the eight life lessons did he demonstrate? How?

   _____

   _____

   _____

6. What challenges did he face? How did he demonstrate the power to choose?

   _____

   _____

   _____

7. How do his challenges compare to your own?

    _____

    _____

    _____

8. What about his story inspired you the most?

    _____

    _____

    _____

David Petite: Create your own reality

1. What influenced David to become an entrepreneur?

    _____

    _____

    _____

2. Which of the eight life lessons did he demonstrate as an inventor and entrepreneur?

    _____

    _____

    _____

3. What challenges did he face? What advantages did he have? How did he overcome his challenges?

    _____

    _____

    _____

4. How did he demonstrate the concept of problems as opportunities?

    _____

    _____

    _____

1. How did he demonstrate an internal locus of control?

    _____

    _____

    _____

2. What did he learn from his failures?

    _____

    _____

    _____

3. How did David create his own reality?

    _____

    _____

    _____

4. How do the challenges he faced compare to your own?

    _____

    _____

    _____

Final Lesson 8 Discussion: Uncle Cleve - Life lessons from an unlikely entrepreneur

As we have seen, Clifton's Uncle Cleve was a man of average means who had no particular advantage over anyone else in his small community. Yet, despite his circumstances and the limitations that were beyond his control, he was able to prosper and thrive.

1. What was it that set him apart?

    _____

    _____

    _____

2. Describe the specific beliefs and assumptions that empowered him to succeed. How were those beliefs and assumptions different from those around him?

_____

_____

_____

3. How was he able to recognize opportunities where others could not?

_____

_____

_____

4. How did he exercise his power to choose? What sacrifices did he make?

_____

_____

_____

5. Do you know of an "Uncle Cleve" in your community? How is his or her story similar? How is it different?

_____

_____

_____

6. How can these lessons be applied today?

_____

_____

_____

Lesson 8: The Power of Persistence - Discussion Notes

_____

_____

_____

_____

_____

_____

_____

_____

_____

_____

_____

_____

Lesson 8: The Power of Persistence - Discussion Notes

_____

_____

_____

_____

_____

_____

_____

_____

_____

_____

_____

_____

Lesson 8: The Power of Persistence - Discussion Notes

_____

_____

_____

_____

_____

_____

_____

_____

_____

_____

_____

_____

_____

Name: _____ Date: _____

Lesson 8: The Power of Persistence - Reflection and Response

Entrepreneurship is not about how to "get rich quick" and expecting it to be easy is a mistake. The secret behind every entrepreneur's success is hard work, perseverance and determination.

Reflection:
Of the eight entrepreneurs featured in this lesson, which inspires you the most? Why? What challenges did the featured entrepreneur overcome? What challenges do you face and how do they compare?

_____

_____

_____

_____

_____

_____

_____

_____

_____

_____

Name: _____ **Date:** _____

Response:
What was the most important aspect of this lesson for you? How will it change your behavior in a way that will move you closer to your goals?

_____

_____

_____

_____

_____

_____

_____

_____

_____

_____

_____

Lesson 8: The Power of Persistence - Application Assignments

Entrepreneurship is not about how to "get rich quick" and expecting it to be easy is a mistake. The secret behind every entrepreneur's success is hard work, perseverance and determination.

By now you have created a personal vision statement that will help you clarify your goals, determine your priorities and decide how you will invest your time and resources.

Prepare your final classroom presentation. Describe your original idea. Describe how your idea evolved through the self-directed learning process. Did you discover another opportunity along the way? Perhaps you have decided that your idea is not worth pursuing. Describe future actions you will take.

Describe the beliefs and assumptions that were challenged. Describe the beliefs and assumptions that were reinforced. Briefly describe the most important thing you learned.

■ How do our choices determine the outcome of our lives?

■ If knowledge and effort (rather than luck or circumstances) are the keys that empower entrepreneurs to succeed, what are you willing to give up in order to accomplish your goals?

■ What can you accomplish through a persistent application of the combining knowledge and effort principle?

As you know, self-directed, life-long learning is the key to success. After the completion of the Ice House Entrepreneurship Program, we encourage you to build on your existing work and to continue the self-directed learning process. And, most of all, you must persevere.

Share your story. Let us know how you are doing and what you are learning along the way. Drop us a note or a video that demonstrates the impact of an entrepreneurial mindset and how it has empowered you to accomplish your goals. Remember, your knowledge, experience and insight can inspire and encourage others who are on a similar path.

Name: _____ Date: _____

ICE HOUSE OPPORTUNITY DISCOVERY CANVAS

Describe the problem being solved or need being fulfilled	Describe your idea for a product or service	Describe solutions currently available

How is your product or service different?	How many people have this problem?	How will you reach potential customers? (marketing & sales)

Why will your customers buy your product or service? (What is your brand?)	How will your customers buy your product or service? (Online, through partnerships with existing business, standalone store)	How can you test these assumptions in the real world? (quickly and cheaply)

CREATING A PERSONAL VISION STATEMENT

The reflection and response assignments have provided an opportunity to reflect on what you have learned and how you can apply the knowledge in a way that will empower you to accomplish your goals. This assignment will enable you to condense the previous assignments into a personal vision statement.

Dare to Dream: Creating a vision statement is a powerful tool, one that separates entrepreneurs from the crowd. A personal vision statement guides your life. It provides a source of inspiration that will energize you. It will help guide the decisions you make and help determine how to invest your time and energy in ways that will lead you closer to your goals.

Without a personal vision, you are much more likely to follow the crowd rather than steering towards a destination of your own choosing. Without a clear vision of where you want to go, it is much easier to squander your time and effort on things that are unproductive and less likely to lead you toward your goals. In fact, research has shown that those who write down their goals are much more likely to accomplish their goals than those who do not.

Creating Your Vision: Find a time and place where you can focus your attention on developing an effective personal vision statement. Write the statements as if you are already making them happen in your life. Try to limit your statement to a single page. And remember, there are no wrong answers.

Commit to Your Vision: Once you have created your vision statement, it is important that you commit to your vision and stay focused on your goals. Share your vision with a trusted friend. Print your vision statement and post it where you can see it often. Include pictures that inspire you.

Describe the future you hope to achieve. Where do you see yourself in 5 years? What obstacles stand in your way? How has this program shifted your perspective? How will you invest your time and energy so that you can accomplish your goals? What is the single most important thing you have learned? What strengths do you see in yourself? How can you use your strengths to accomplish your goals? What weaknesses do you see in yourself? How can you compensate for your weaknesses so that you can accomplish your goals? How will an entrepreneurial mindset enable you to accomplish your goals?

Name: _____ Date: _____

PERSONAL VISION STATEMENT:

_____

_____

_____

_____

_____

_____

_____

_____

_____

_____

_____

Name: _____ Date: _____

PERSONAL VISION STATEMENT:

_____

_____

_____

_____

_____

_____

_____

_____

_____

_____

_____

_____

Name: _____ Date: _____

PERSONAL VISION STATEMENT:

_____

_____

_____

_____

_____

_____

_____

_____

_____

_____

_____

Name: _____ Date: _____

ICE HOUSE OPPORTUNITY DISCOVERY CANVAS

Describe the problem being solved or need being fulfilled	Describe your idea for a product or service	Describe solutions currently available

How is your product or service different?	How many people have this problem?	How will you reach potential customers? (marketing & sales)

Why will your customers buy your product or service? (What is your brand?)	How will your customers buy your product or service? (Online, through partnerships with existing business, standalone store)	How can you test these assumptions in the real world? (quickly and cheaply)

Name: _____   **Date:** _____

ICE HOUSE OPPORTUNITY DISCOVERY CANVAS

Describe the problem being solved or need being fulfilled	Describe your idea for a product or service	Describe solutions currently available

How is your product or service different?	How many people have this problem?	How will you reach potential customers? (marketing & sales)

Why will your customers buy your product or service? (What is your brand?)	How will your customers buy your product or service? (Online, through partnerships with existing business, standalone store)	How can you test these assumptions in the real world? (quickly and cheaply)

ICE HOUSE OPPORTUNITY DISCOVERY CANVAS

Describe the problem being solved or need being fulfilled	Describe your idea for a product or service	Describe solutions currently available

How is your product or service different?	How many people have this problem?	How will you reach potential customers? (marketing & sales)

Why will your customers buy your product or service? (What is your brand?)	How will your customers buy your product or service? (Online, through partnerships with existing business, standalone store)	How can you test these assumptions in the real world? (quickly and cheaply)

Name: _____   Date: _____

ICE HOUSE OPPORTUNITY DISCOVERY CANVAS

Describe the problem being solved or need being fulfilled

Describe your idea for a product or service

Describe solutions currently available

How is your product or service different?

How many people have this problem?

How will you reach potential customers? (marketing & sales)

Why will your customers buy your product or service? (What is your brand?)

How will your customers buy your product or service? (Online, through partnerships with existing business, standalone store)

How can you test these assumptions in the real world? (quickly and cheaply)